HOW TO
FLYFISH

from newcomer to *improver*

John Symonds

MERLIN UNWIN BOOKS

First published by Merlin Unwin Books, 2014

Merlin Unwin Books

Palmers' House, 7 Corve Street,

Ludlow, Shropshire, SY8 1DB

www.merlinunwin.co.uk

A CIP record of this book is available from the British Library.

Designed by John Symonds

www.fly-fish-guide.net

Printed and bound by Great Wall Printing

ISBN 978-1-906122-63-8

HOW TO
FLYFISH

from newcomer to
improver

About the author

JOHN SYMONDS (pictured on the left) is a keen flyfisherman and fishes for salmon, trout and grayling in the Wye and Usk catchments as well as the Welsh borderlands. He decided to become a certified casting instructor and guide as a retirement occupation and has successfully qualified to Advanced Professional Game Angling Instructors (APGAI) single- and double-handed levels, and is an International Federation of Fly Fishers (FFF) Two-handed Casting Instructor (THCI).

John's other interests include photography and graphic design and so this book has been an opportunity to use these to convey the basic skills required by flyfishers in most branches of the sport.

This book is a companion to another book written by the author and a fellow guide, Philip Maher, called *Flycasting Skills for beginner and expert*, also published by Merlin Unwin Books. A third book is being written, which will cover the basic fly-tying skills and this will complete the trilogy.

This book is dedicated to my mother
Molly Symonds 1926–2013

Contents

Passing it on   1

BASIC SKILLS   2
Connecting backing to the reel   4
The Grinner Knot   5
Connecting fly-line to backing   6
The Nail Knot   7
Assembling a fly-rod and line   8
Threading the fly-line   9
Whipped Loop (fly-line to leader)   10

STILLWATER LURE FISHING   12
The trout's food   13
Locating lake trout   14
Essential stillwater patterns   16
Landing a trout   17
The Blood Knot (fly to leader)   18
Tying the fly to the leader   19
Making a Braid Loop   20

RESERVOIR BOAT FISHING   22
Flat wing flies (Diptera)   23
Locating fish from a boat   24
Choice of tactics   26
Controlling the drift   28
Controlling the drift with the paradrogue   29
Essential boat patterns   30
Fishing at different depths   31

Leaders and droppers   32
The Davy Knot (hook to leader)   33
Figure-of-Eight Loop (leader to fly-line)   34
Figure-of-Eight Dropper   35

DRY FLY FISHING   36
Upwinged flies (Ephemeroptera)   37
Essential dry fly patterns   38
Presentation of the dry fly   39
Where river trout lie   40
Constructing a tapered leader   41
The Double Blood Knot   42

NYMPH FISHING   44
A typical nymphing rig   45
Essential nymph patterns   46
Leader lengths for nymphing   47
Reading the river   48

FISHING THE CADDIS IMITATION   50
Caddisflies (Trichoptera)   51
Essential caddis patterns   52
New Zealand style   53

FLY CASTING   54
The roll cast   55
More casting skills   56
The lift and overhead cast   57

Drag-free drift	58	Salmon fly-line options	71
Methods of presenting the fly	59	Double Turle Knot (salmon fly to leader)	72
		Shooting heads	74
TENKARA	60	Skagit lines	75
Tenkara rods	61	The Welded Loop	76
Typical Tenkara rigs	62		
The Tenkara set-up	63	LEADERS	78
Essential Tenkara fly patterns	64	Leader selection	79
Finding the fish Tenkara-style	65		
		SAFETY CHECKLIST	80
SALMON FISHING	66	Bibliography	86
Essential salmon patterns	67		
Locating salmon in rivers	68	INDEX	86
Salmon fishing styles	70	Further reading	88

Passing it on

When I first took up flyfishing I had no previous experience to draw from, but I read books and magazines avidly in an attempt to gain the knowledge that I so desperately needed. It became immediately apparent that flyfishing was a multi-faceted discipline with many challenges requiring various skills.

My early days on the rivers and reservoirs were on the whole fruitless but this didn't deter me and because there was that suicidal fish that would, just once in a while, impale itself on my hook. This was enough to keep me going. There was always this overwhelming urge to crack the magic code that would make me a great flyfisher, like the well-known anglers who wrote the articles for the flyfishing magazines. However, the more I read, the more I became confused.

On the whole, fishermen are very generous in sharing their knowledge and killer fly patterns, even though this is often misguided and embroidered – no-one likes to admit that they cannot catch fish. However, very occasionally, they do offer a nugget of information, which can be helpful in the quest for continual improvement.

I believe that many game anglers, like me, live an unfulfilled dream, even though they have invested in the best tackle that money can buy, carry thousands of flies around with them and have read all the books.

Gradually, I am getting closer to fulfilling my own dream but often it seems that when I am just about to close in, and become accomplished, the fish are playing to a new set of rules. We flyfishers console ourselves by learning to cast, visiting far-flung fishing destinations, buying a few days on prime beats or watching DVDs of experts landing large fish. This keeps the dream alive.

Fortunately, as I widened my horizons, I came across flyfishermen who were able to impart basic skills and tips on watercraft to me.

Suddenly, I made a mega leap and I started catching fish, including salmon, with increasing regularity. Had I arrived? No, a few lean spells to brought me back to reality, and left me with a need to try and make some sense of my plight. This is how it is with flyfishing and, in my opinion, the reason the sport is so compelling.

Eventually, I considered that I had enough flyfishing knowledge to become a guide and instructor, and so this is what I do nowadays. I am surprised how difficult it is for beginners to find information on the basic skills, even in these days of mass communication, and how I have to start from scratch with many of my clients. I also have to attend to the needs of my good fishing friend, Michael, and point him in the right direction so that he has a greater chance of catching fish. Consequently, I have become aware of recurring themes and the essential skills that flyfishers need but may not be aware of. This book is a record of the demonstrations and explanations that I have used countless times as a professional guide. I think this approach is unique because I haven't come across anything quite like it myself.

Also, the book has been compiled as a series of projects, which I hope flyfishers will enjoy doing and find rewarding. Many parents who have enjoyed flyfishing will want their children to have the same magical experiences and I hope that this book will provide a pathway for them too.

We are all seeking contentment in life and flyfishing is one of the ways of achieving this goal. It can be practised in solitude or as a group, it is a great leveller and a source of continuous enjoyment. I hope you get as much fun from reading this book as I have had in writing it.

John Symonds, June 2014

BASIC SKILLS

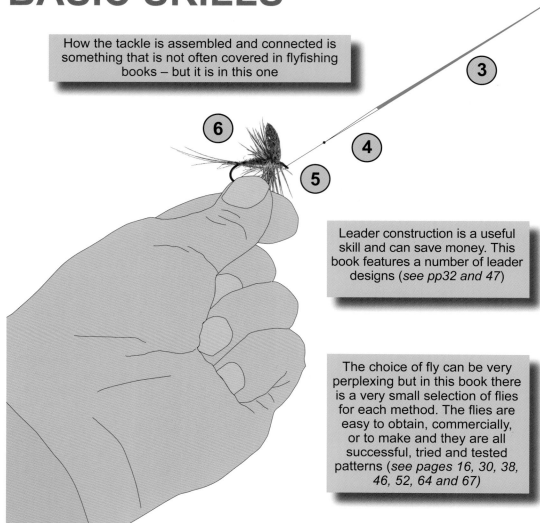

How the tackle is assembled and connected is something that is not often covered in flyfishing books – but it is in this one

③

⑥

④

⑤

Leader construction is a useful skill and can save money. This book features a number of leader designs (*see pp32 and 47*)

The choice of fly can be very perplexing but in this book there is a very small selection of flies for each method. The flies are easy to obtain, commercially, or to make and they are all successful, tried and tested patterns (*see pages 16, 30, 38, 46, 52, 64 and 67*)

The tackle you will need for most methods of Western flyfishing include the following items:

① **A fly-reel** which is used to store backing and the fly-line. The fly-reel usually has an adjustable drag system. A drag system provides controlled resistance whilst playing the fish, without applying too much pressure which could result in the leader breaking and loss of the fish.

The fly-line is wound onto a spool, which can be removed and replaced with a spare, carrying a different type of fly-line. On the base of the reel housing there is a foot which fits into the reel seat, located in the butt of the fly-rod.

② **A fly-rod**, which is made from carbon fibre for lightness, strength and flexing ability. It is normally assembled by inserting the tip of one section inside the next smallest and firmly pushing them together. The rod has a number of rings that allow the fly-line to run smoothly from the reel to the rod-tip.

2

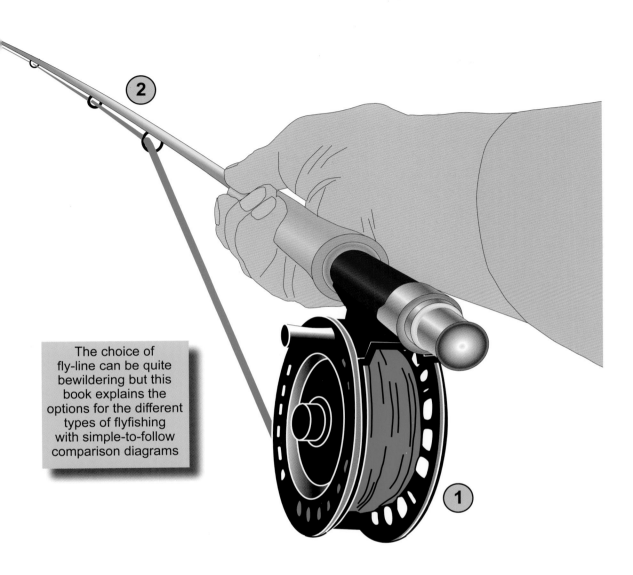

The choice of fly-line can be quite bewildering but this book explains the options for the different types of flyfishing with simple-to-follow comparison diagrams

3 **A fly-line** with a weight that matches the fly-rod, made from a braided core that is coated with PVC or polymer. The front end of the fly-line is tapered to provide a good turnover and delicate presentation of the fly.

4 **A tapered leader** is usually at the end of the fly-line and this is made from either monofilament, copolymer or fluorocarbon to provide strength combined with a very fine diameter that is less likely to spook fish.

5 **A tippet** (a length of straight nylon) is connected to the leader to provide a gentle presentation of the fly. This can be replaced when it becomes worn or too short.

6 **Flies** are imitations of the natural insect, made from fur, feather and other synthetic materials, or they simply give a general impression of a food item that is attractive to fish.

3

Connecting backing to the reel

Before the fly-line is attached to the reel it is advisable to wind on a fairly long length of backing braid, so that the fly-line is not coiled too tightly onto the spool and winds onto the reel quicker. More importantly it allows the fly-line to run off the spool when playing a particularly strong, fighting fish such as a salmon. The breaking strength of the backing must be suitable for the size of fish that will be caught but 20lb is normally the minimum rating.

TIP

The amount of backing can be estimated by temporarily attaching the fly-line to the spool with masking tape and winding it on. The space remaining between the fly-line and the outer peripheral cage of the reel can be measured and this can be used to determine the depth of backing that is required on the reel.

1 The diagram on the opposite page shows how the backing can be connected to the fly-reel by using a grinner knot.

2 Start by threading the braid between the spool and the reel cage. Wrap the braid twice around the spool and bring it out on the opposite side to where it enters. The free end is known as the 'tag end'.

3 Make a loop in the tag end and offer this up against the main length of braid which is still on the bobbin. The latter is referred to as the 'standing end'.

4 Make four loops of the tag end over both the loop and the standing end.

5 Pull the loops tightly, by using the tag end, so that they form a slip knot. Check that they sit down cleanly, butting up against each other, without any overlap.

6 Pull the standing end of the backing to partially close the loop down onto the spool.

7 Before closing the loop down completely onto the arbor of the spool, cut off the tag end with a pair of sharp scissors.

8 Finally push the knot down onto the arbor, whilst pulling the standing end, to tighten it up.

The backing is now connected and is ready for winding onto the fly-reel. It is important at this stage to decide whether a right- or left-hand wind is preferred. This will determine the direction in which drag is applied (to resist the pull of the fish when it is running). In the opposite direction of rotation there is no drag because it is not required when the fly-line is retrieved by winding it back onto the reel.

As the backing is wound on it should be guided onto the spool to ensure a uniform distribution and a flat surface to wind the fly-line onto.

The knot that is used in this method for connecting the backing to the reel is known as the grinner, which makes a very useful loop with a slip-knot and it has a number of other fishing applications. For instance it can also be used for attaching a fly to a leader. If the knot is not tightened down, the small loop that passes through the eye of the hook will allow the fly to move freely and hence it will be more attractive to fish.

Another knot in this family, the double grinner, provides a neat way of joining two lengths of monofilament, with different diameters, for making a tapered leader.

A rotating connection for a dropper can be constructed from a loop made with a grinner, which can be located between two joints in a leader, and tightened down to provide a rotating, tangle-free, connection.

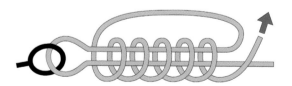

The grinner knot

The Grinner Knot (connects backing to reel)

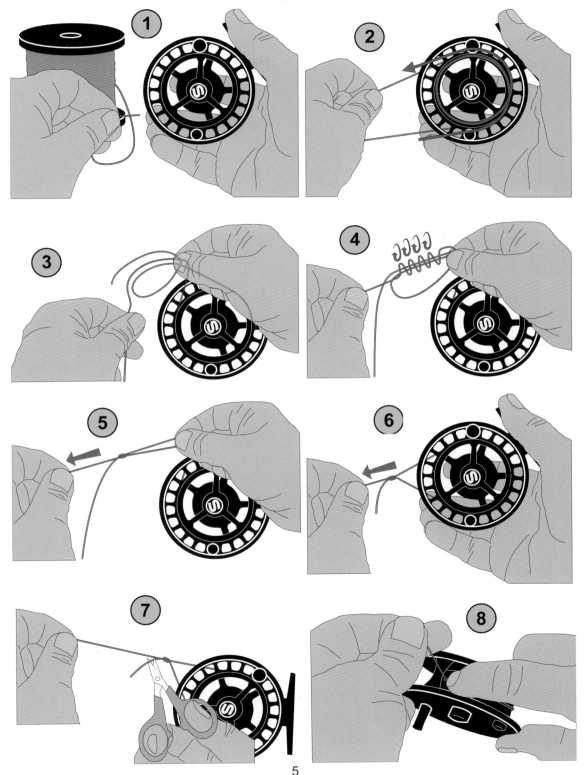

Connecting the fly-line to backing

A new fly-line from the factory is normally wound onto a spool and has a free end that is tagged with a label saying 'reel this end'. The backing that has already been put onto the spool has to be attached to this end and an effective way of doing this is to use a nail knot.

The diagram on the facing page shows how the backing is joined to the fly-line by using a nail knot that is tied with the help of a darning needle.

1 Firstly, grasp the very end of the fly-line, with the needle lying alongside it and the eye of the needle protruding out from the front end of the fly-line. Then grasp the tag end of the backing and hold it in the position where the nail knot is to be started. This should be slightly back off the end of the fly-line to allow for four turns of backing and some clearance at the end so that the finished knot is not accidently pulled off the fly-line when it is tightened down.

2 Next pull the tag end of the backing under the needle and fly-line and over the top.

3 By pinching the windings as they are formed, this frees up the other hand to continue pulling the backing round and under for the next turn. This sequence is repeated until four turns have been applied.

4 The tag end can now be threaded through the eye of the needle, whilst the windings are held in place with the other hand.

5 Whilst continuing to hold the windings firmly in place, the needle is withdrawn though the loops, pulling the tag end with it. Continue to pull the needle until the tag end drops free.

6 For the next step, make sure that the fly-line is supported, to prevent it sliding out of the loosely-wound turns, and then seize both sides of the backing and tighten down the nail knot. Make sure that the knot pulls down neatly, with touching but not overlapping turns.

7 Holding the backing and fly-line and pulling tightly will cause the nail knot to bed down into the coating of the fly-line and this will also allow the strength of the connection to be tested.

8 Cut off the tag end with scissors.

There are some alternative methods that can be used for tying this knot, such as using a short loop of monofilament instead of a needle. Alternatively, the windings can be made on a small diameter, rigid tube and the tag end threaded through this before it is withdrawn.

The nail knot is also a useful method for joining a leader onto a fly-line because this gives a good transference of energy and helps with the turnover, and hence presentation of the fly.

Once the fly-line has been connected to the backing it can be wound onto the reel. It is helpful if the fly-line spool can be allowed to rotate on a pencil, or something similar, which is held by an assistant.

It should be possible to guide the fly-line onto the reel by manipulating it with the finger and thumb of the hand that supports the reel. This will ensure that the fly-line sits uniformly on the reel without any high spots that could possibly jam against the reel cage.

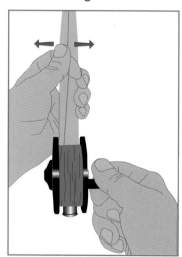

Usually the fly-line manufacturer provides a detachable, self-adhesive label with the line details on the spool, which can be stuck to the fly-reel as a reminder, for when the reel and line is stored with a number of others.

The Nail Knot

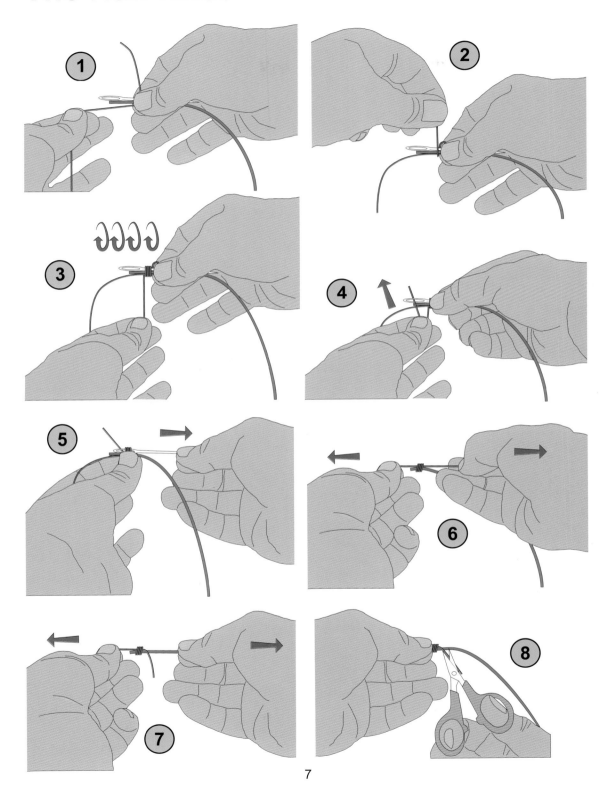

Assembling a fly-rod and line

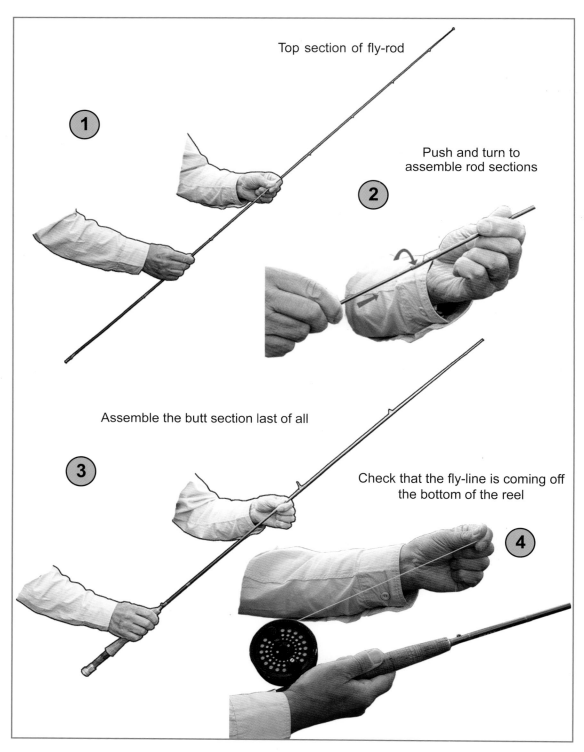

Top section of fly-rod

1

2 Push and turn to assemble rod sections

Assemble the butt section last of all

3

4 Check that the fly-line is coming off the bottom of the reel

Threading the fly-line

When assembling a fly-rod it is easier to start from the tip section and to work down.

Hold the tip section in one hand and present the next section up to the ferrule located at the bottom of the tip with the other hand. Check that the rod-rings are roughly in line.

1 Push the lower section into the tip section, firmly but not forcefully, twisting the bottom section as it locates and lining the rings up at the same time. Often there are markers on each adjoining section of the rod to assist with alignment.

2 Repeat the procedure and finally fit the butt section to the rest of the assembled fly-rod.

3 Place the fly-reel in the reel seat and tighten up the threaded rings, which hold the reel foot in place. Check that the fly-line is coming off the bottom of the reel and facing towards the first stripper-ring on the fly-rod.

4 To avoid the ingress of grit and dirt into the moving parts of the reel mechanism it is advisable to pull a few feet of fly-line off the reel and to leave it in coils on the ground, in a relatively clean area.

5 Next take the tip of the fly-line, double it over and holding the loop that is formed, between the thumb and forefinger, feed this through the rings starting at the first stripper ring at the butt end of the rod and through each ring, in turn, to the rod-tip. This will ensure that if the line accidently slips through the fingers, it will not run back down the rings again, causing some annoyance and the need to thread the line again.

Once there is a foot or so of fly-line outside the rod-tip it is quite a simple matter to swing the fly-rod from side to side and to feed out more of the fly-line between the thumb and forefinger of the non-casting hand, until sufficient fly-line is outside the rod-tip.

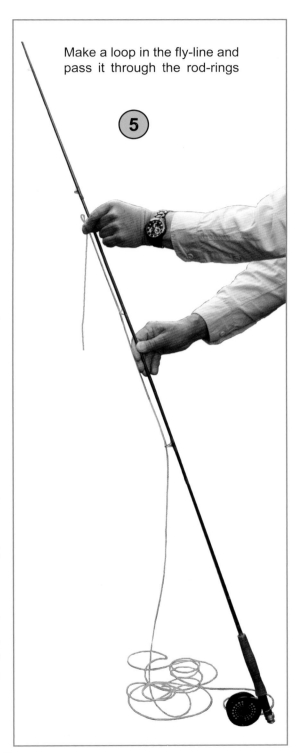

Make a loop in the fly-line and pass it through the rod-rings

5

Whipped loop (links fly-line to leader)

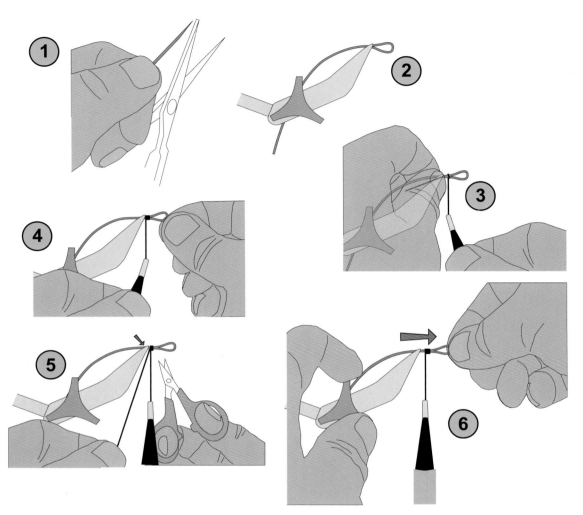

One of the neatest ways of making a loop in the end of a fly-line, for a loop-to-loop connection to the leader, is to use a fly-tying vice and a whipping tool.

1 First of all cut the very end of the fly-line, at an angle, to make a nice, long taper. This will be butted up against a parallel section of the line and will provide a smooth transition from the main line, without any unsightly lumps.

2 Then fold the end over to make a compact loop and clamp the very end of the overlapping section in a vice.

3 Next start winding on a few loose turns of thread, catching the tag end in so that it is locked.

4 Now wind on a few more turns, using the free hand to support the loop, so that the turns can be made tighter by applying more pressure.

5 Cut off the tag end with a pair of scissors.

6 Reposition the loop in the vice so that the remainder of the loop is exposed and can be whipped.

7 Complete the whipping by lifting the thread up from the front and over the

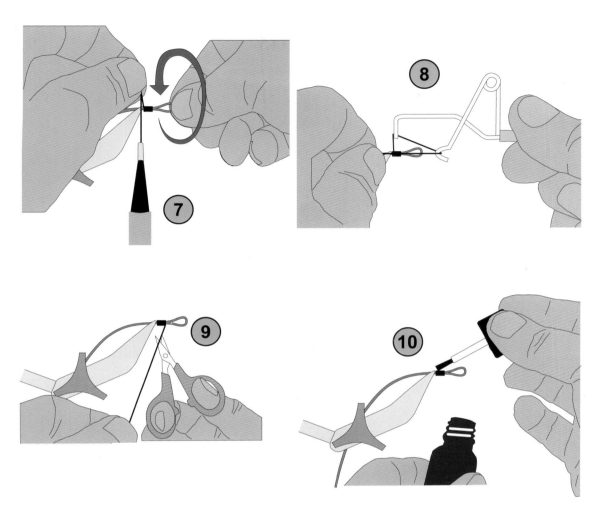

loop, letting it drop on the other side. Position each turn of the thread so that it touches against the previous one.

8 When all of the loop joint has been neatly covered with thread, finish off by applying 5 turns with a whip-finishing tool. Alternatively, the final turns can be hand whipped.

9 Cut the thread close to the last turn.

10 Apply a coating of varnish, or UV-setting gel, to the whippings so that they are held permanently in position but still have a degree of flexibility.

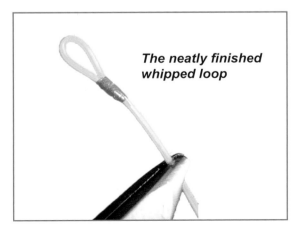

The neatly finished whipped loop

11

STILLWATER LURE FISHING

Many anglers are first introduced to the sport of flyfishing at their local stillwater lake, which is regularly stocked with rainbow trout up to a few pounds in weight and also has stocked or natural brown trout. Most fisheries of this type have a policy that caught fish must be taken (except brown trout) and this ensures a good turnover of fish but some do exercise a catch and release policy.

Stillwater fisheries are ideal for the beginner because fishing is usually from the bank or platforms and there is normally good access to the taking fish. Furthermore the fisheries are often open all year round and so this provides opportunities for the avid flyfisher to continue his sport, throughout the winter months.

Casting a fly to the fish is not a major challenge and so basic casting skills are normally sufficient for achieving some degree of success. Fellow anglers are only too happy to pass on advice on the choice of fly and successful tactics and so this is a good and enjoyable way of learning for the beginner.

Basic Tackle Requirements

- ☐ #6 9ft fly-rod
- ☐ Cassette type fly-reel
- ☐ #6 weight forward floating fly-line
- ☐ #6 intermediate fly-line
- ☐ #6 sinking fly-line
- ☐ Spool of fluorocarbon or monofilament leader – 8lb breaking strain
- ☐ Forceps
- ☐ Priest
- ☐ Marrow spoon for sampling fish stomach contents
- ☐ Line snips
- ☐ Landing net with a long handle
- ☐ Fly floatant
- ☐ Polaroid glasses
- ☐ Bass bag for keeping fish
- ☐ Waterproof clothing
- ☐ A fishing bag for storing the tackle
- ☐ A selection of lures

The trout's food

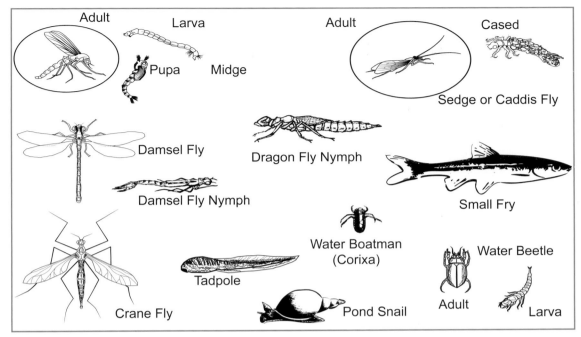

Adult — Larva — Pupa — Midge

Adult — Cased — Sedge or Caddis Fly

Damsel Fly

Dragon Fly Nymph

Damsel Fly Nymph

Small Fry

Crane Fly

Tadpole

Water Boatman (Corixa)

Pond Snail

Water Beetle — Adult — Larva

A healthy stillwater will have well-oxygenated water, preferably stream-fed, and lots of plant life, which support all manner of creatures that trout feed on.

Amongst the most prolific are midge larvae, especially during the colder months, and they make up the major part of the stillwater trout's diet. These are bottom-dwelling and exist in many colours such as black, grey, fawn, green and red (the latter known as bloodworm by anglers). Subsequently, the larvae will make their way to the surface of the water as pupae and emerge as adults. All of these stages in the midges' life cycle are of interest to anglers and there are many fly patterns which imitate the naturals – *see section on reservoir fishing*.

The trout may also feed on aquatic snails, despite their hard shells, especially during the spring and autumn when there is a scarcity of other food. Snails normally live in weed beds but in the summer months as the water becomes warmer the snails may float to the surface and hang for long periods in the surface film, which makes them an easy target for foraging fish.

Also in the summer the damsel and dragon fly nymphs are very active and can be found around the margins, amongst weed beds, where they live. Trout are more likely to feed on damsel nymphs, which are very easy to imitate by the flyfisherman.

Other favourite foods include small fish (fry), which swim in shoals and tend to be eaten by rainbow trout, particularly the larger ones, in the autumn months. Small roach, perch, bream or sticklebacks are the most common species found in stillwaters and are easy to mimic with a lure. Pin fry are present throughout the year and often a small fry pattern will bring success to the angler.

When the crane flies (or daddy-long-legs) are hatching, usually when there is a damp spell of weather in the late summer, they can be seen flying haphazardly and landing on the surface of the water, where they are readily taken by trout and this can be a time of good sport for the flyfisherman.

There are numerous other aquatic and terrestrial species that trout will feed on, including tadpoles, corixa (water boatmen), ants, caddis larvae and water beetles.

Locating lake trout

For the beginner it is best to fish with a single fly on a 12ft leader, made from 8lb breaking strength monofilament or fluorocarbon. If fish are taking flies from the surface of the water then a floating line will be the obvious choice. However if fish cannot be seen feeding then searching tactics have to be employed which involves the use of an intermediate or sinking fly-line which will get the fly down deeper.

1 If there is a wind blowing then there will be a good chance that the fish will be on the down-wind side of the lake because the natural food will be blown in this direction. This rule does not always apply if there is a sufficient supply of food in other parts of the water but it is a good starting point.

2 Weed-beds and drop-offs are good places to try and this means that the fish could be in the margins, close to the bank. The weed-beds are a natural habitat for insects and other aquatic species, providing both microscopic food and protection. The fish will patrol the fringes of the weed beds on the look-out for food. Drop-offs occur where the shallow area near the shore suddenly falls away into deep water.

3 By preference trout feed off surface food when it becomes available, normally starting in the early summer. It is obvious when fish are top-feeding because they disturb the surface water, often accompanied by a distinct splashing noise. In such situations a floating line with a long leader and a dry fly such as a hopper or sedge pattern is the obvious choice. Retrieval of the fly may not be necessary so initially it can be left static and if this does not work then various retrieval methods can be tried: slow stripping or figure-of-eight methods for instance. Often, a fly which is skating across the surface and creating a wake can be irresistible to fish and so this can

be worth a try. Sometimes the fish will take the emerging insect subsurface and so the rise form is more subtle and a Shuttlecock Buzzer or a Klinkhamer might be more successful in coaxing the fish to take.

4 Strong sunlight and warm weather put the fish down and they do not feed on the surface. Alternatively, there may be no hatching flies or sufficient food in the top water so the fish might be foraging at depth. This being the case the choice of an intermediate or sinking fly-line and a searching pattern, such as a lure, will be more fruitful. A good system is to time the sink by counting: a low count at first and gradually increasing until the correct depth is found by hooking a fish. This time delay can then be repeated with a good chance of catching more fish.

With a sunken line the speed of retrieval is dictated by the need to avoid catching weed in the bottom of the lake in which case the fly will be hovering just over the likely fish feeding areas and will have a good prospect of being taken. It is advisable to fish right into the margins and then to lift the fly slowly because this is usually when following fish will strike to avoid the prey from escaping, so the final part of the retrieve should not be rushed and a slight pause, before the final lift, might just induce the fish to take.

5 When there is overhanging shrubbery or trees, there is a good chance that terrestrial insects will fall accidently into the water where they are seized upon by fish. This can be a good place to cast and to present the fly so that it lands heavily on the water, thus attracting fish.

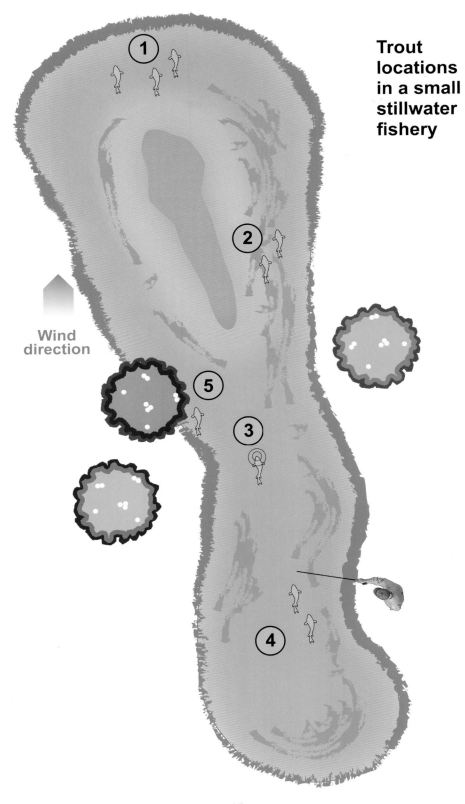

Trout locations in a small stillwater fishery

Wind direction

Essential stillwater patterns

Damsel Nymph
Hook: Size 8-10 long-shank with gold-plated brass bead
Thread: Fluorescent-green 8/0
Tail: Olive marabou
Body: Olive ostrich herl
Rib: Fine silver wire
Hackle: Grey partridge
Head: Prominent fluorescent green covered with clear varnish.

Cat's Whisker
Hook: Size 8-10 long-shank
Thread: White 8/0
Tail: White marabou
Body: Fluorescent yellow chenille
Rib: Silver oval tinsel
Wing: White marabou

Muddler Minnow
Hook: Size 8-10 long-shank
Thread: Brown 8/0
Tail: Turkey feather slip
Body: Gold tinsel
Head: Clipped deer's hair
Wing: Turkey feather slip

Viva
Hook: Size 8-10 ordinary, long-shank or small double
Thread: Black 8/0
Tail: Fluorescent green floss or wool
Body: Black chenille
Rib: Silver tinsel
Wing: Black marabou or squirrel hair
Cheeks (optional): Jungle cock

Daddy Longlegs
Hook: Size 8 long-shank
Thread: Brown 8/0
Body: Pheasant tail fibres
Legs: Knotted pheasant tail fibres
Hackle: Furnace cock
Wing: Grizzle hackle tips

Flies tied by Giuliano Masetti

Landing a trout

When a fish takes, the angler will sense this by a tugging on the fly-line or by a splash or swirl on the surface and the first objective is to set the hook in the fish, by lifting and pulling back the fly-rod quickly, keeping tension on the fly-line. The fish will react, running in the opposite direction to which it is restrained.

The fish should be allowed to take line in a controlled manner, either off the reel with drag applied or by feeding line between the fingers, thus avoiding any breakage of tippet or leader.

Often when the pressure is taken off the fish it will tend to settle down and then the fly-line can be gently retrieved. The angler has the option of putting the stripped line on the ground or back onto the reel, which is much neater and allows more movement up and down the bank, whilst keeping the fly-line clean.

It may be necessary to allow the fish to run and take line several times before it begins to tire. Once it no longer offers any resistance, the fish's head can be lifted out of the water which will reduce its ability to use its body power to hamper retrieval.

In readiness for landing the fish, the net should be placed in the water so that the fish can be guided towards the rim of the net without frightening it. Then you lift the rod-tip and scoop the net under the fish.

Once netted, the fish can be lifted out onto the bank for removal of the hook or for despatching, depending on whether the fishery allows catch-and-release or not.

Clean the net by dipping it in the water, removing any slime or debris, and then place it on the bankside ready for further use.

The Blood Knot (for fly to leader)

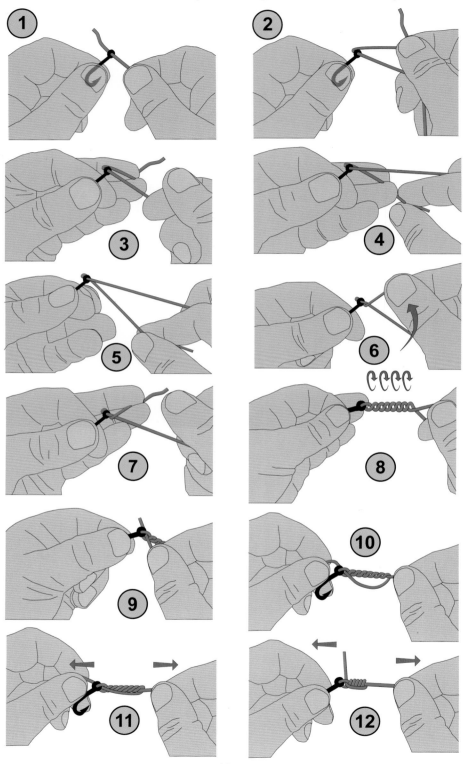

Tying the fly to the leader

One of the most common knots in flyfishing is the blood knot and this can be used for attaching the fly to the leader. It is a very simple knot to tie as shown in the sequential diagram shown on the facing page.

1 Hold the hook between the finger and thumb of one hand with the eye of the hook exposed. Taking the end of the leader in the other hand push the tag end through the eye.

2 Pull a reasonable working length of leader tag end through the eye of the hook.

3 Pick up the tag end with the first and middle fingers of the hand holding the hook and take it around the back of the standing end of the leader.

4 Now pick up the tag end with the other hand again.

5

6 Continue to pass it around the leader.

7 Pick the tag end with the first and middle fingers of the hand holding the hook again.

8 Repeat the above sequence so that there are four turns of the tag end wrapped around the leader standing end.

9 Take the tag end and pass it through the gap between the first turn and the hook eye.

10 Pull the tag end through the gap.

11 Apply tension by pulling the tag end and standing end in opposite directions. This will cause the knot to tighten up.

12 Grasp the hook and the standing end of the leader and pull in opposite directions to lock the knot in place.

Cut off the tag end with a sharp pair of scissors.

Tucked Blood Knot *(see below)*

There is a variation of this knot which is called the Tucked Blood Knot, which is designed to prevent the tag end from slipping through the gap between the hook eye and the first turn when extreme tension is applied to the leader when a fish is 'on'.

To tie this knot the initial sequence is the same as that for the blood knot but before the knot is tightened down, the tag is passed through the loop *(after Step 10)* that is formed between the last and first turns, when the tag end is brought back over the knot.

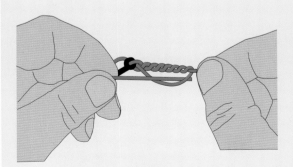
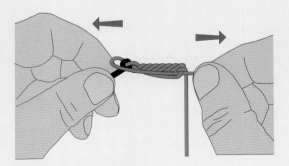

Optional steps instead of 11 for the Tucked Blood Knot

Making a Braid Loop (an easy loop for the stillwater angle

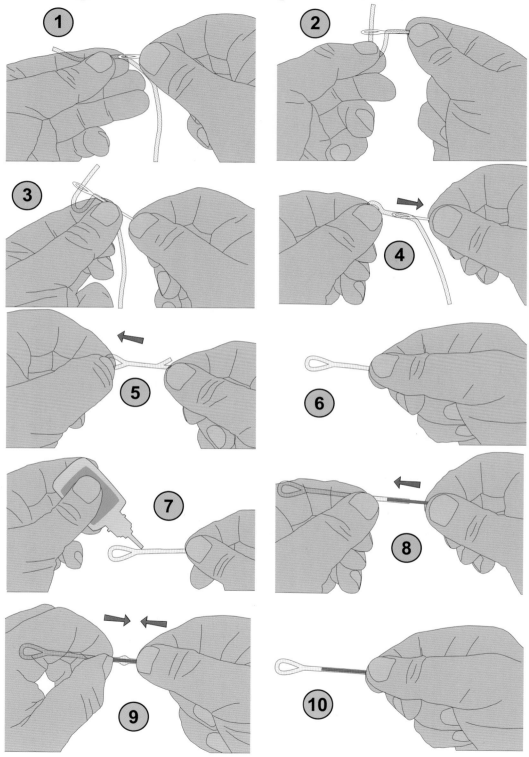

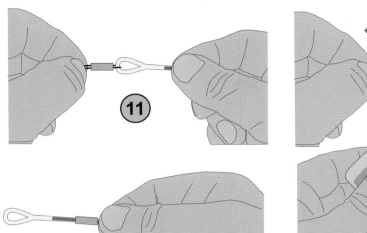

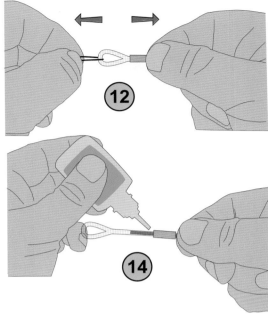

1. Cut off a length of braid approximately 6ins (150mm) long and insert the eye end of a darning needle into the middle of the braid approximately 2ins (50mm) from the end.

2. Thread the needle through the braid and insert the loose end through the eye of the needle.

3. Grasp the section of braid over the needle between the forefinger and thumb.

4. Pull the needle back down through the braid and form a loop. Continue pulling until the end of the braid comes out through the side of the standing end and the needle can be removed, leaving a tag end.

5. Pull the loop so that the tag end is just pulled back inside the main section of braid and a neat loop is formed.

6.

7. Apply a small blob of superglue to the section of braid just below the loop junction. The glue will be sucked in due to capillary action and so apply with care.

8. Insert the end of the fly-line into the open end of the braid.

9. Push the braid over the fly-line until the butt of the fly-line is right up against the loop. The braid can be eased onto the fly-line by holding the open end of the loop and compressing a short section of braid by pushing the loop end with one hand and then releasing the other hand, and repeating this process as necessary.

10. The loop is now fitted onto the fly-line but requires locking in place and to do this a short length of silicon tube, with a small diameter is used.

11. Take a short-length monofilament and pass it through the loop. Slip the length of silicon tube over the monofilament.

12. Pull the silicon tube so that it slips over the loop and is pulled down to the end of the braid.

13.

14. Now apply a small blob of superglue to the end of the silicon tube. This will wick up through the whole length of tube and form a strong joint.

RESERVOIR BOAT FISHING

Photo by Peter Wyles

Loch-style fishing from a boat, on one of the numerous reservoirs with a nice breeze and a gentle wave, natural flies are rising to the surface in readiness for hatching into adults – it is at this time that they are most vulnerable and easy prey for feeding trout.

When the flies are ready to hatch they change from larva into pupa and make their way up to the surface where they emerge as adult midges, mosquito-like and with wings. During their journey from the bottom of the reservoir to the surface they are picked off by trout.

Flyfishers refer to midges as buzzers.

This chapter of the book is dedicated mainly to the various methods of buzzer fishing from a drifting boat but it also offers advice on alternatives that might be more applicable on the day, depending on conditions.

Basic Tackle Requirements

- ☐ #6 9ft fly-rod
- ☐ Cassette type fly-reel
- ☐ #6 weight forward floating fly-line
- ☐ #6 intermediate fly-line
- ☐ #6 DI3 sinking fly-line
- ☐ #6 DI5 sinking fly-line (optional)
- ☐ #6 DI7 sinking fly-line (optional)
- ☐ Spool of fluorocarbon leader – 8lb breaking strain
- ☐ Paradrogue
- ☐ Forceps
- ☐ Priest
- ☐ Marrow spoon for sampling fish stomach contents
- ☐ Line snips
- ☐ Landing net
- ☐ Fly floatant
- ☐ Buoyancy aid
- ☐ Polaroid glasses
- ☐ Bass bag for keeping fish
- ☐ Waterproof clothing
- ☐ A fishing bag for storing the tackle

Flat wing flies (Diptera)

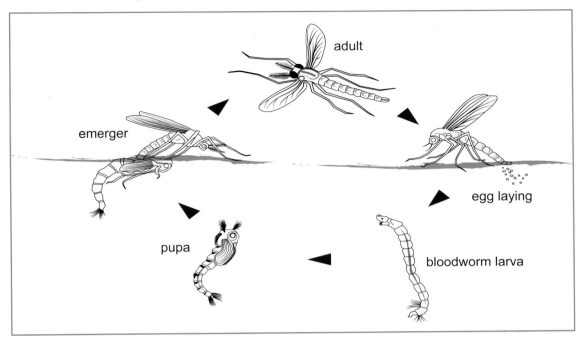

adult

emerger

egg laying

pupa

bloodworm larva

Chironomids or midges are the most prolific of insects in trout waters and the Black Buzzer imitation of the midge pupa is probably the most successful fly for reservoir fishing, throughout the season but the best months are from early April till June. It can be fished static in sunny, calm conditions, from a long leader on a floating line. In breezier conditions the buzzer can be suspended from droppers, washing line style, with a booby on the point and either a floating or a sinking line.

Another equally successful fly is the Diawl Bach (little devil) which is more of a general insect imitation but seems to work best when trout are feeding on midge pupae.

The Claret Hopper is normally fished as a dry fly, representing the adult midge. It works well when there are good waves rolling across the surface of the water, throughout the fishing season but mainly in May and June or September and October, when the weather remains settled. Sometimes the fly will also be very effective in catching trout when it is fished on a sinking line and slowly retrieved.

Midges begin life as larva, often referred to as bloodworm by anglers, which are freely floating and live in weed beds, silt and sand, near the bottom of the water. When fully grown they pupate and rise to the surface within a few days and so can be found at almost any depth but prior to emergence they hang vertically below the surface of the water. Often they can become trapped in the surface film when the water is calm.

During emergence the midge expands by pumping haemoglobin, which causes it to split out of its pupal shuck. The fishing imitations are often tied with pronounced segmented bodies and bright red ribbing. The adult midge then takes to the air for mating. Afterwards the females return to the water to deposit their eggs.

At this stage the laying female is called a 'buzzer', so called by anglers because of the noise it makes when flying.

Locating fish from a boat

The main challenge with boat fishing is locating where and at what depth the fish are feeding. What they are feeding on is not quite so important because it is always possible to fish with lures, which attract fish without imitating their food.

One easy way of finding fish is to trail a sinking line behind the drifting boat, with a lure attached, and to gradually increase the depth at which it is fishing, in areas where the fish could be shoaling. Some fisheries may not allow this method, which is called trolling, and it certainly isn't permitted in competitions, so check the rules beforehand. It is also possible to use this technique by casting over the front of the boat, providing it is anchored or not drifting too quickly.

Initially, the vastness of water in large reservoirs can be overwhelming to the uninitiated but there are a number of likely fish-holding areas that can be identified, as shown in the diagram opposite.

(1) Dam walls can offer rich pickings to feeding trout because they provide shelter and a plentiful supply of terrestrial insects which have fallen into the water. Invertebrates will also cling to the stonework below the waterline.

(2) Likewise strong winds can blow insects from trees and shrubs growing along the bankside onto the water. When banks are on the downwind side of the reservoir the currents can transport food into the shallows.

(3) Weed beds support insect life and provide cover. Normally these can be found at the edge of a shelf, where the depth of water rapidly drops. This is an ideal location for finding fish.

(4) Prominences and bays will attract fish because of converging currents, which will concentrate drifting food, and the close proximity of deep water.

(5) Foam lanes are caused where two circulating currents meet and create the bubbles of foam on the surface. These areas trap insects and this attracts fish. Adjusting the drift of a boat along these feed lanes can be very successful. Likewise, aerators that are used by the reservoir management to increase oxygen levels in the water can attract fish, especially in hot weather.

(6) Feeder streams running into the lake provide oxygenated water and a constant supply of food from upstream.

(7) During the late spring and early summer it is worth prospecting the deeper water, where the fish might be feeding sub-surface on daphnia or insect larvae and emergers.

Playing a rainbow trout

When a fish has been hooked most anglers immediately and intuitively strike to set the hook. The fish should then be allowed to run, taking fly-line, but kept under control by maintaining tension on the fly-line. The fish will often go deep and try to get under the boat.

As the fish begins to tire, at each opportunity the line should be wound back onto the reel, which has been set with a loose drag. At this stage the fish may still make unexpected runs and so if necessary the line should be allowed to come off the reel again if there is a risk of breaking the leader.

Eventually, it should be possible to lift the fish's head out of the water, so that it will no longer have a purchase on the water with its fins and so will be easier to manoeuvre. Place the net in the water in readiness without risk of spooking the fish and prolonging the fight. The fish can then be pulled to the side of the boat and scooped up with the net.

Where to find trout on a larger water

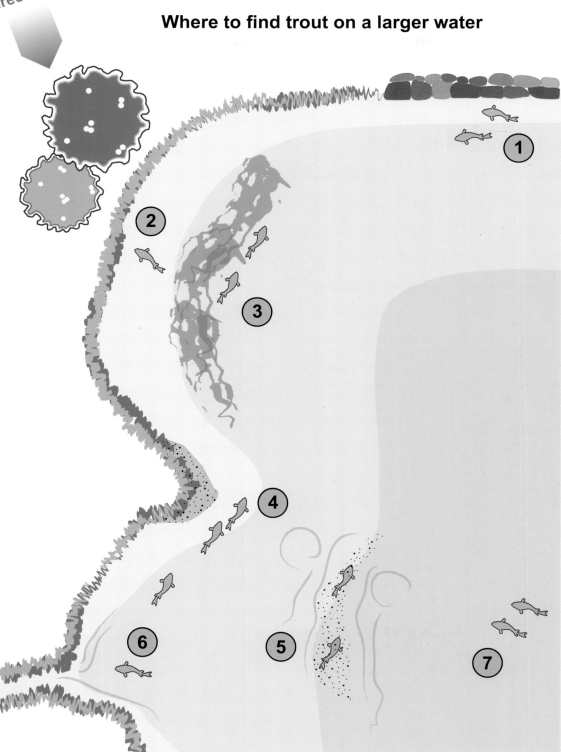

Choice of tactics

Reservoir flyfishing success is greatly dependent on experience, fishing the same waters frequently and the ability to switch tactics quickly. However, this should not deter the beginner because acquiring these skills can be very satisfying.

Considering the various influencing factors will greatly improve the odds of catching fish.

Prior knowledge
With the wealth of information now available on the internet it is possible to obtain reports on virtually every fishery, with locations where fish have been caught and the fly patterns that have been used. This intelligence, together with up-to-date information provided by the fishery manager, will help considerably in determining where and how to start the day's fishing.

Weather
Before leaving home, or even a few days before the fishing day, it is worthwhile checking the weather forecast for wind speed and direction, the prospects of possible cloud cover or sunshine, air temperature and pressure. All of these can be used to decide on the most suitable style of fishing.

Seasons
The time of year has a great effect on where the fish will be and what they will be feeding on. **During the spring** the water temperature will be low and very few insects will be hatching. Fish congregate in the shallows, around the margins and will most likely be taking midge larvae, which are present throughout the year and can even hatch out during the winter.

An intermediate fly-line (very slow sinking) should be suitable because the water will not be deep and most of the feeding will be just sub-surface. However, if the weather is cold and windy the fish may be down on the bottom of the reservoir and so it might be worthwhile trying a slow sink line if the intermediate line doesn't work. Buzzers, nymphs and gold-headed patterns that imitate the chironomids (midges) will probably work well.

As the water temperature rises in **late spring and early summer** there will be a greater variety of fly life and the fish will be more active, possibly taking fly close to the surface and so emerger patterns or dry flies are worth trying. Alternatively, the washing line method with two nymphs on the droppers and a booby on the point may coax fish that are feeding on rising pupae. If these methods fail then a team of nymphs on a sinking line might work better.

When the fish are **showing on the surface** then obviously top of the water tactics are more likely to catch fish.

During **high summer**, the fish could be at any depth depending on the light intensity and water temperature. On very warm, bright days it might be better to fish deep, with three nymphs on a sinking line. However, when the sky is overcast and there is a stiff breeze, which generates nice rolling waves, these might be the ideal conditions for fishing with a claret hopper.

At the **end of the season** the fishes' diet can change to corixa and fry, which live predominantly in the shallows and so concentrating on these areas with suitable imitations is worthwhile. There are no hard and fast rules, observation of fish activity and identification of hatching insects or their shucks must be maintained at all times, for gathering visual clues and narrowing down the choice of tactics.

Time of day
Reservoir fishermen know that fish behaviour is constantly changing, almost minute by minute, throughout the day. Quite often the fish can be feeding high in the water during the early morning and then go down deep through the middle of the day and then back up to the top in the evening. Therefore, the angler must be prepared to switch tactics when a successful method stops working. The time of day will also influence the hatching times of insects and there is often a magic hour in the afternoon when there is a lot of surface activity.

Sedges, meanwhile, are known to hatch during the evening hours.

Light intensity

Fish are more likely to take a fly when cloud passes in front of the sun and they will suddenly switch off when the sun comes out again. In early autumn, as the angle of the sun is lower, there are more opportunities for finding fish near to the surface. When the sun is high, overhead, in mid-summer, this is the time when the fish seek the protection from its glare, in the depths of the reservoir. This is when fast sink tactics are employed.

Water temperature

As water temperatures rise, the fish become more lethargic.

In large reservoirs the water will stratify and the fish will tend to gravitate to a certain depth, called the thermocline, where the deep water that is low in oxygen meets the warm top layer.

Daphnia, minute water fleas, congregate in blooms or clouds that move in the water and change depth depending on temperature. Trout will gorge on these and this is often evident when a fish is spooned to show that they are full of a daphnia jelly, which can be green or red and has the consistency of wallpaper paste. This is probably why the orange and green fritz material used in blob patterns is so successful, as is the green wool used in the Viva and Cat's Whisker lures.

Fishing depth

As we have seen, many of the above factors influence the depth at which the flies are fished. One way of fishing deeper is to use heavier flies but this is not permitted in competition fishing and so sinking lines have been developed for this purpose. The choice of sink rate is straightforward when fishing from an anchored boat but it is more complicated when the boat is drifting because the depth will be determined by the wind speed, boat speed controlled by a drogue and the line retrieval rate. Certainly, it is important to keep in touch with the flies so that any takes can be sensed at the finger tips but then the fish might be attracted by slow or fast moving flies depending on what they are feeding on at the time. Another technique is to move the flies rapidly over a very short distance and then pause. Competition anglers will often strip a sinking line back very quickly with a single lure, like a large blob, attached the leader. This will certainly attract stocked fish but is unlikely to work on the more educated, mature specimens.

Retrieval

The speed of retrieval will affect the depth at which the flies are fished, ranging from static (deep) to fast (surface – depending on the sink rate of the fly-line). Retrieval can also be used to impart a particular movement to the flies, for instance a constant jerking motion created by a figure-of-eight method or a raise-and-lower motion caused by short pulls with stops in between them.

Choice of leaders

To avoid leader breakages it is advisable to fish with a leader that has an 8lb breaking strength – maybe 6lb if the fish is played carefully. Reservoir fish can fight hard and so in any case it is better to let the fish run when it wants to and to retrieve line onto the reel when the tension reduces. A long leader with a thin diameter is less likely to deter wary fish.

...and finally, when all the thinking and pondering has been done, you can get out on the water and put theory to practise!

Controlling the drift

When fish have been located then the appropriate tackle is selected so that the line will hold the flies at the correct depth, and will compensate for the speed at which the boat is drifting. If there is no wind or a very gentle breeze then it is just a question of choosing a fly-line which provides the required sink-rate – or the rate of retrieval can be changed to control the fishing depth.

Higher wind speed is more of a problem because when a boat sits in the water its prow is higher than its stern and so the area exposed to the wind is greater at the front end of the boat than the rear. Furthermore there is a greater area below the waterline towards the back of the boat, and the propellor is submerged, causing more drag on that side. Consequently the boat will not drift straight, causing the fly-line of the angler sitting on the stern side to drift in front of the angler on the prow side, which means it is difficult for the latter to retrieve the fly-line without causing a tangle.

The speed of the drift can be slowed down by the use of a drogue, which is like an underwater parachute tethered to the back of the boat. The direction of the drift can also be controlled if a paradrogue with two cords, is used (*see diagram*). Adjustment of the cord lengths will determine the direction in which the boat drifts. It is often desirable for this to be parallel with the bank.

Another tactic is to drift the boat so that it approaches the bank on the downwind side of the reservoir where the fish are more likely to be feeding because the wind will blow food items to that side.

A paradrogue will collapse when one of the cords is pulled into the boat

and this is essential when fishing close to the bank because you can then quickly turn the boat around and motor back out to start a new drift. Retrieve the drogue as you start to motor across the reservoir, so that it doesn't become tangled with the propellor.

On the following page there is a diagram showing one possible method of adjusting the drogue cords to achieve drift in any direction irrespective of the wind direction.

One simple way of adjusting the length of the paradrogue cords is to cut them and insert cleats that are used for tensioning the guidelines on larger tents. These provide a means of disconnecting and resetting the cords very quickly and with fine adjustment. The cord on the left hand side is shortened to make the boat drift to the left and the one on the right hand side to drift to the right.

The end connected to the boat can be attached to G-clamps or a carabiner which is used to secure the cord around the boat seat or to the gunwales.

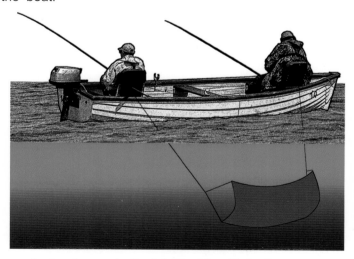

A steady, controlled drift with a little directional 'steer' is possible with the aid of a paradrogue

Controlling the drift with the paradrogue

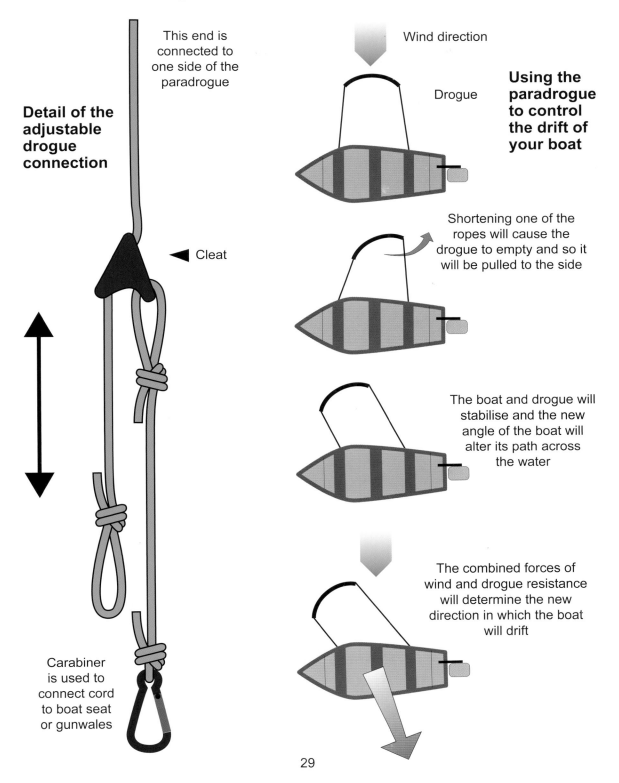

This end is connected to one side of the paradrogue

Wind direction

Drogue

Using the paradrogue to control the drift of your boat

Detail of the adjustable drogue connection

◀ Cleat

Shortening one of the ropes will cause the drogue to empty and so it will be pulled to the side

The boat and drogue will stabilise and the new angle of the boat will alter its path across the water

Carabiner is used to connect cord to boat seat or gunwales

The combined forces of wind and drogue resistance will determine the new direction in which the boat will drift

Essential boat patterns

Black Buzzer
Hook: Size 10 heavyweight down eye
Thread: Black 8/0
Rib: Red holographic tinsel
Wing buds: Mirage tinsel
Coating: Varnish or UV curing resin

Diawl Bach
Hook: Size 10 heavyweight down eye
Thread: Black 8/0
Tail: Brown cock hackle fibres
Body: Peacock herl
Rib: Red holographic tinsel
Beard: Brown cock hackle fibres

Hot Pink Booby
Hook: Size 10 heavyweight down eye
Thread: White 8/0
Tail: Hot pink marabou
Body: Pink fritz
Eyes: Shaped from pink Plastazote cylinders
Epoxy stick-on eyes optional

The Blob
Hook: Size 10 heavyweight straight eye, wide gape
Thread: White 8/0
Tail: Strands mirage tinsel
Body: Yellow and orange fritz

Claret Hopper
Hook: Size 10 heavyweight down eye
Thread: Black 8/0
Body: Dubbed claret seals fur
Rib: Pearl tinsel
Legs: Knotted pheasant tail fibres
Collar Hackle: Brown cock hackle

Fishing at different depths

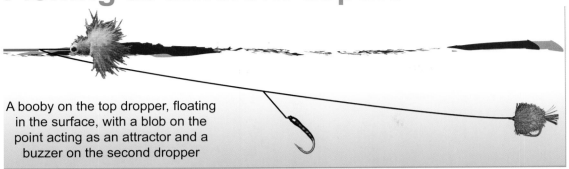

A booby on the top dropper, floating in the surface, with a blob on the point acting as an attractor and a buzzer on the second dropper

Floating fly-line

Fishing 'washing line style' with the booby on the point

Buzzer and Diawl Bach hanging below the surface

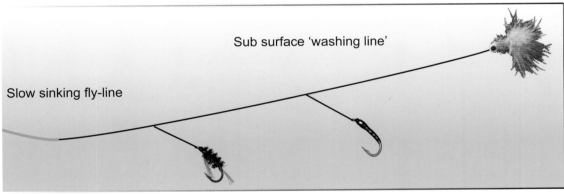

Sub surface 'washing line'

Slow sinking fly-line

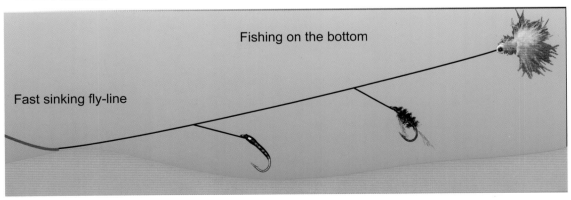

Fishing on the bottom

Fast sinking fly-line

Leaders and droppers

When fish are feeding, time is of the essence and so anglers have developed knots than can be tied quickly even in windy conditions. On the following pages are three knots that are based on the figure-of-eight principle. These are ideal for fluorocarbon because there are a fewer number of turns and the strain is usually taken by a double thickness of leader, which makes the knots much stronger and more dependable.

The Davy knot *(see opposite)* was created by Davy Wotton and maintains around 100% breaking strength. It is used for tying the fly onto the leader and it is much smaller than most other knots so it does not impede the action of the fly as it swims in the water. Furthermore, there is less waste with a Davy knot (unlike a blood knot, for instance) because with practice the tag can be kept very short. So your dropper lasts longer due to less wastage when flies are frequently changed.

So that the strength of the whole leader is not compromised when droppers are used, it is important to have the droppers attached as short lengths to a single length of leader that runs from the point to the loop connection. This is normally 18 feet long and is measured by pulling three lengths off the spool, with the arms completely outstretched (approximately 6 feet from finger tip to finger tip). A **water knot** (also called a surgeon's knot) will suffice but this involves putting three or four lengths of long leader through a loop, which isn't the easiest

thing to do in a high wind. On the other hand a **figure-of-eight dropper knot** *(page 35)* only requires one pass of the leader through a loop during its formation, which is both quick and easy to accomplish.

The short length of leader that is used for making the dropper should be approximately 12 inches long to avoid the annoyance of creating a dropper that is too short.

A **loop-to-loop** connection is an easy way of joining a leader to the fly-line which has a welded loop, usually factory-constructed at the time of manufacture. Loops are not only strong but they allow a quick changeover of leader when there is a tangle. There are other types of loop but the figure-of-eight is one of the easiest to tie and it is very dependable.

This family of knots is recommended for use with 8lb breaking strain fluorocarbon. The latter has been selected for this method of fishing because it is heavier than water and after a short while it will sink more readily, providing a better presentation of the flies.

It is advisable to pull the knots together slowly to avoid overheating caused by friction and hence a resulting deterioration of the knot's strength. Some anglers use saliva or knot lubricant to give a stronger and more compact knot.

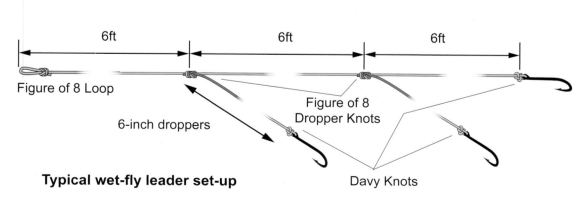

6ft   6ft   6ft

Figure of 8 Loop

6-inch droppers

Figure of 8
Dropper Knots

Typical wet-fly leader set-up

Davy Knots

The Davy Knot (connects hook to leader)

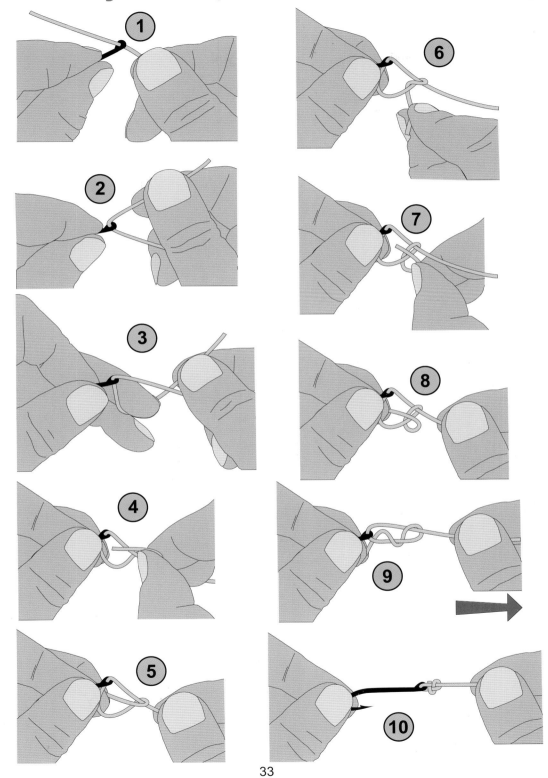

Figure-of-Eight Loop (for leader to fly-line)

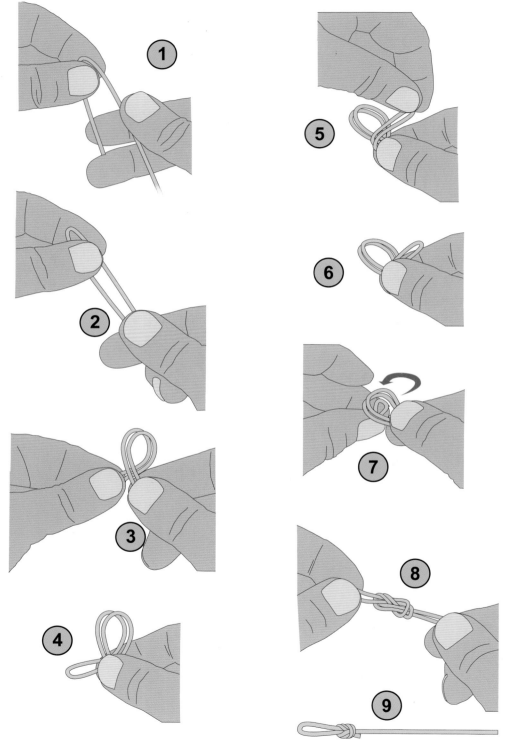

Figure-of-Eight Dropper

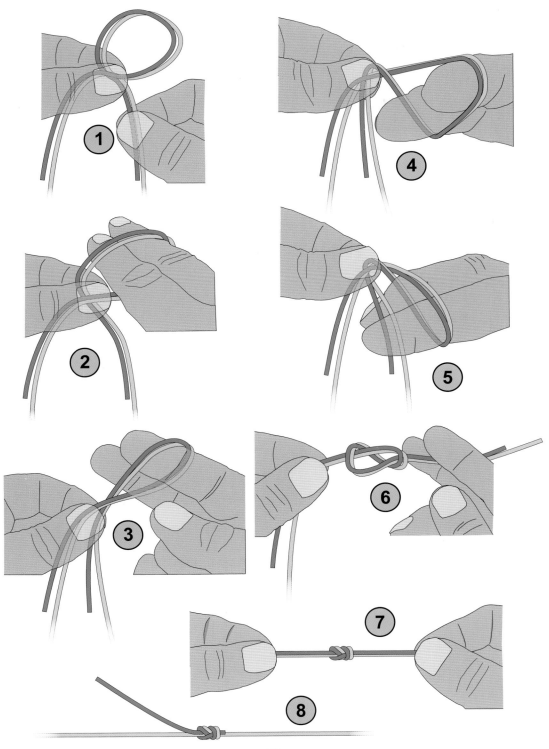

35

DRY FLY FISHING

For many flyfishers, the ultimate experience is to successfully take a fish, in the river, with a dry fly imitation that they have made themselves. Often the fish are rising to a hatch of flies and can be seen taking them off the surface of the water from the same spot. Larger fish often push small fish off the prime feeding positions, which are close to an area of refuge and safety.

It is a good strategy to sit and observe the river before starting to fish, noting where the fish are rising before wading into the water. The fish can be targeted so that the closest ones can be caught first without spooking the others further upstream. The angler should always be aware of where other fish are showing.

To catch a fish with a dry fly, it is essential that the fly is presented gently, a foot or so upstream of the fish, so that the fly floats over the fish with a drag-free drift. To prevent the fly-line from pulling the fly and causing it to skate across the surface of the water it is necessary to put slack into the fly-line during the cast.

The choice of fly is important because ideally it should match the natural insect on which the fish are feeding, although this may not be immediately obvious if several different types of fly are hatching simultaneously. Often a generic pattern can be used to solve this problem. The fish may be scrutinising the shape of the fly on the water – as well as the colour. If the fish refuses to take after a few casts with a particular fly, it may be worthwhile trying another pattern or another hook size. Often the fish can be feeding on extremely small insects or taking them sub-surface.

Basic Tackle Requirements

- ☐ #5 9ft fly-rod
- ☐ #5 9ft floating, double-taper, fly-line (weight forward is also acceptable)
- ☐ #5 9ft fly-reel
- ☐ 12ft 5x (4lb breaking strength), nylon tapered leader for dry fly fishing
- ☐ Spool of 5x tippet
- ☐ Multi-compartment fly-box with spring lids (or similar)
- ☐ Forceps
- ☐ Line snips
- ☐ Landing net
- ☐ Fly floatant
- ☐ Polaroid glasses
- ☐ Waders
- ☐ Wading jacket
- ☐ Fishing hat or baseball cap

Upwinged flies (Ephemeroptera)

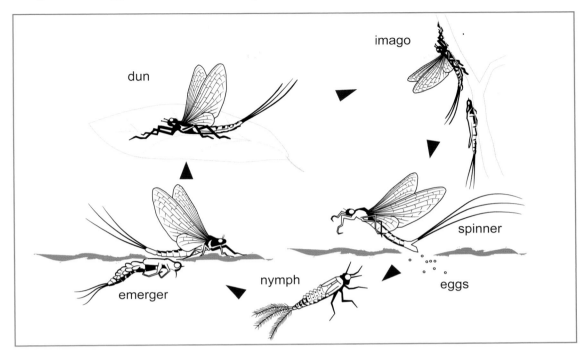

Mayflies epitomise the sport of flyfishing, with their upright wings, often two large ones and two spur wings, in various colours: yellow, brown, olive and blue being typical and two or three long graceful tails.

All upwing flies (including mayflies) begin life as eggs which, after approximately two weeks hatch into nymphs. They have an external skin which acts as a skeleton and, periodically, they moult and grow a new skin.

Nymphs can be found clinging to stones, rocks or aquatic plants on the river bed, where they feed on decaying vegetable matter and some species can be carnivorous. They have a head, thorax, segmented abdomen and six legs. Down each side of the body there are rows of gills which pulsate in a rhythmical fashion. At the front of the head are two antennae.

It can take up to twelve months for the nymph to become fully grown, when it rapidly makes its way to the water's surface where it splits out of its case and emerges as a winged insect, dull in colour and called a dun. The emerged insect will sit on the surface whilst its wings dry and it summons up the strength to fly off. Some species choose to emerge by climbing up aquatic vegetation.

Certain warm conditions will trigger the emergence of many nymphs simultaneously and they may be seen coming off the water in swarms. This is referred to as a 'hatch' by anglers.

Duns, which are also called sub-imagos, are characterised by their long tails and translucent wings and they are dull in appearance. For a period, which can be as long as 36 hours for some species, they hide in vegetation until they are ready for their final transformation into an imago or spinner, when they are ready to mate. At this stage they emerge from their old skin, with shiny bodies, bright wings and very long tails. They can be observed flying in swarms, mating in the air and finally dropping down onto the surface of the water to deposit eggs.

Afterwards both the males and females die, many of them falling onto the water, again provoking a frenzy from feeding fish.

Essential dry fly patterns

Greenwell's Glory
Hook: Size 14-16 dry fly
Thread: Yellow or primrose 8/0
Rib: Fine gold wire
Body: Well-waxed yellow or primrose tying silk
Wing: Starling or mallard primary
Hackle: Furnace cock hackle

Grey Duster
Hook: Size 10-16 dry fly
Thread: Grey
Tail (optional): Badger cock hackle fibres
Body: A blend of bluish-grey rabbit underfur and guard hairs
Hackle: Well-marked badger cock

Orange Quill
Hook: Size 12-16 dry fly
Thread: Orange
Tail: Natural red cock fibres
Body: Stripped peacock quill dyed hot orange or dark orange
Wing: Pale starling set upright
Hackle: Natural dark red cock

Adams
Hook: Size 8-22 medium to lightweight dry-fly
Thread: Black or brown 8/0
Tail: Grizzle and brown cock hackle fibres
Body: Grey rabbit or muskrat underfur
Wing: Grizzle hackle points
Hackle: Grizzle and brown cock hackles

Royal Wulff
Hook: Size 10-18 dry fly
Thread: Brown or black 8/0
Tail: Brown deer body hair
Body: Peacock herl with a band of red floss silk in the centre
Wing: White calf tail, upright and divided
Hackle: Dark brown cock

Flies tied by Michael Wardle

Presentation of the dry fly

Unless the dry fly is presented with a drag-free drift, it is unlikely that the fish will take it. The exception to this is a sedge imitation which is allowed to skate across the water – just like the natural.

In order to present the fly delicately, the front end of the fly-line has a taper. The fly-line generally terminates in a loop and this is used for attaching a leader, which provides a continuation of the line taper. The leader has three sections; a butt, a taper and a tippet and for general river fishing a length of approximately 9ft should be adequate. The butt diameter should not be less than 60% of the diameter of the fly-line tip.

Continuous tapered leaders are commercially available, but some anglers prefer to make their own from different diameters of monofilament, to suit their own particular fishing needs. Manufactured tapered leaders are expensive so it can be worthwhile attaching a length of tippet to the end and this can be replaced when it becomes worn or too short.

Connection from the fly-line to the leader can be loop-to-loop or permanent, by using a nail knot, for instance. The loop at the end of the fly-line can be made by heat-welding, whipping or attaching a ready-made braided loop.

If you have fly-tying equipment, the whipped loop is easy to make, is by far the neatest and lifts off the water cleanly at the end of the drift, unlike the braided loop which sticks to the water.

Drag-free drift can be achieved in a number of ways depending on casting restrictions and how the fly is to be presented. Often the speed of the flowing current differs between where the angler is standing and the target fish, in which case a mend (some slack) is required to prevent the fly-line from pulling the fly round too quickly.

Casting directly upstream can reduce the effects of drag but there is always the chance that the fish will be spooked as the fly-line drops over it. A better approach is to cast diagonally, upstream, in front of the fish, across the river. In this way, when the fly lands it will travel a lot further on the surface, without drag, hence increasing the chances of raising a fish.

The length of fine tippet at the end of the leader can also be used to good advantage because if it can be made to fall on the water in loose curves rather than under tension, then there will be a short period when the fly will be floating dead drift and has more chance of being taken. There are a number of different slack-line casts that can be used to achieve such a presentation.

Sometimes a downstream cast can be effective and drag-free drift is achieved by putting a series of wiggles in the line, before it drops on the surface of the water.

It is advisable to treat the dry fly with floatant just as soon as it is tied on, before fishing. This will help it to repel water and maintain buoyancy. There are a number of proprietary liquids, gels and powders available for this purpose.

Where river trout lie

The main concerns of river trout and grayling are to protect themselves from predation, to feed and to conserve energy.

To achieve these aims, the larger fish will hold premium positions close to the river bank, where there are overhanging bushes or tree roots, where insects are likely to float by, so that they can dart out quickly when they see suitable food items. Trailing water plants also offer cover.

When there are large rocks in the river there is usually a fast and deep stream of water running to one side of them. The fish will lie in the shelter of the rock and swim out to take a natural or artificial fly.

Often fish can be located in the seam of water that lies between fast flowing and slack water. This usually occurs at the tail of a pool where the water runs into a distinct channel and there is often a deep hole at the end of it that has been scoured out in times of flood. This can be a prime taking spot.

It is always worthwhile fishing the tail of a pool on the lip of the 'V' that concentrates the flow of water into the channel below because this creates a natural food conveyor and the fish will lie there.

Sometimes, when they are feeding, trout will hold station in the food stream and rise to insects as they float downstream towards them, making an easy target for the fly angler. The fish will leave a safe position to feed in the food lanes but will immediately bolt back to shelter if they are spooked or hooked.

When they are feeding on duns the fish will make a decision whether or not it is worth expending energy to intercept the food item and they'll weigh up their chances of success before making a move. They are more likely to take an emerging fly than one that is fully hatched, sitting on the surface of the water and ready to fly away in the next instant.

So in essence, it is essential to read the water and to imagine the path in which the flow of water will funnel the food items and the suitable places nearby where the fish will lie for easy interception.

It is also important to remember that the fish will be facing the opposite direction to the prevailing current, which doesn't necessarily mean upstream. The current might be flowing across the river or stream, or even upstream in an eddy, and so the fly should be presented accordingly.

The prime positions and feeding lanes are easier to spot in freestone rivers because they are spring-fed and height is subject to the amount of rainfall. Chalkstreams on the other hand have a fairly stable water level because the water seeps from the water table through the ground so there the main characteristics might be weed beds and overhanging vegetation.

As a rule of thumb it is best to fish with the dry fly where the water level is less than knee deep because it is more likely that the fish will decide that the energy used in rising to the surface is less than that gained from eating. Conversely, in water that is waist high, or deeper, it is more likely that the fish will feed on nymphs rather than waste energy rising to the surface.

On hot, sunny days, the fish are more likely to find deep pools and it will be more difficult to coax them to the surface, unless there is a big hatch of flies on which the fish can feed continuously. Therefore, the use of searching tactics may prove fruitless. Fishing in shady areas, under vegetation, will almost certainly prove to be more rewarding (see also pages 48-49).

Constructing a tapered leader

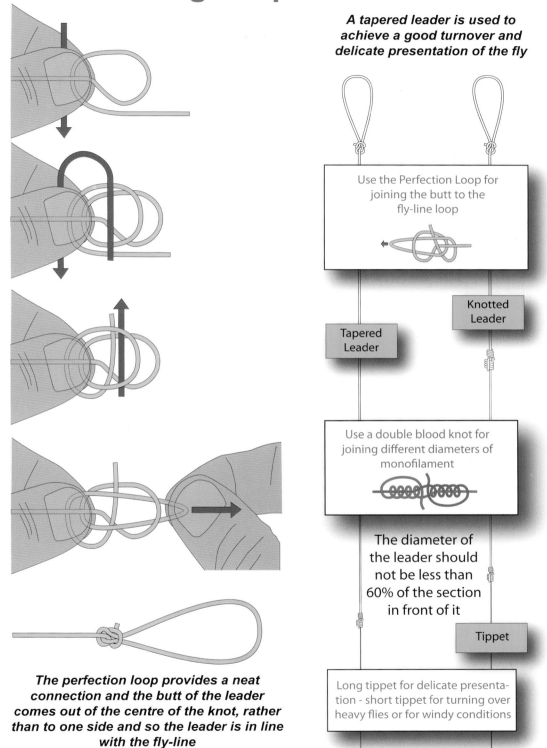

A tapered leader is used to achieve a good turnover and delicate presentation of the fly

Use the Perfection Loop for joining the butt to the fly-line loop

Tapered Leader

Knotted Leader

Use a double blood knot for joining different diameters of monofilament

The diameter of the leader should not be less than 60% of the section in front of it

Tippet

Long tippet for delicate presentation - short tippet for turning over heavy flies or for windy conditions

The perfection loop provides a neat connection and the butt of the leader comes out of the centre of the knot, rather than to one side and so the leader is in line with the fly-line

41

The Double Blood Knot...

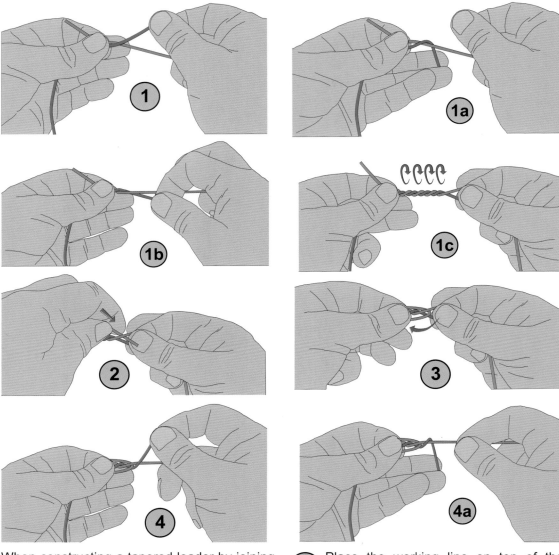

When constructing a tapered leader by joining together lengths of monofilament, the double blood knot can be used to make a strong, neat connection, with lines of different diameters. The sequence on these two pages shows how to tie the knot in an uncomplicated manner.

For ease of explanation we will call the green coloured line the static line and we will call the blue coloured line the working line.

1 Place the working line on top of the static line and wind it around the static line four times.

2 Insert the static tag end where the two lines separate at the end of the four turns.

3 Grip the static tag end and the four turns together so that the static tag end cannot move.

4 Continue to put a further four turns of the working line onto the static line.

...for joining lines of different diameters

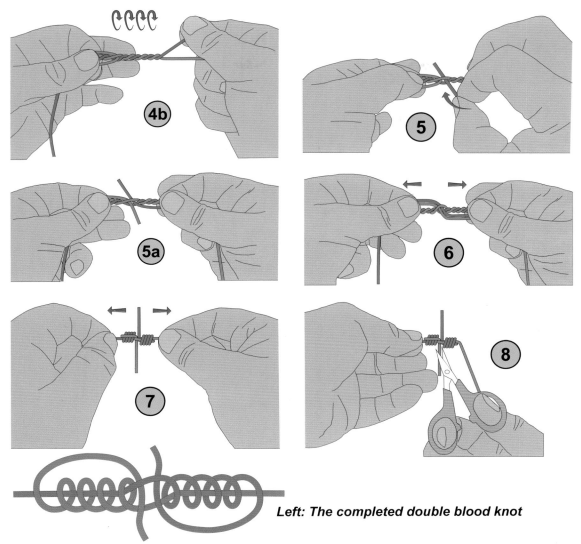

Left: The completed double blood knot

5 Now insert the working tag end through the gap that has been created where the static tag end passes between the two sets of turns. Make sure that the working tag end points in the opposite direction to that of the static tag end.

6 To close the knot, grasp the tag ends in each hand between thumb and first finger. Each tag end should be on the same side as its corresponding standing end. By pulling the hands apart the knot will close up.

7 Check that the knot is correctly seated with uniform (but not overlapping) turns. Apply some knot lubricant and pull the standing ends in opposite directions to complete and lock the knot.

8 Snip off the tag ends with a pair of sharp scissors. One tag end may be left for use as a dropper, if required. The selected tag end should be the one which faces in the direction of the point end (thinnest diameter) of the tapered leader.

NYMPH FISHING

There are a number of techniques for fishing with nymph patterns, in rivers and streams. Eastern European flyfishers have developed very successful methods that have now been adopted more-or-less worldwide by devotees. These involve suspending a team of nymphs below the rod-tip and guiding them downstream.

A heavy nymph is tied onto the bottom dropper and the weight of this fly is carefully selected so that it matches the depth of water and current flow and so bounces along the riverbed as the rig is let downstream from the rod-tip.

A second nymph is tied onto a dropper so that it hovers just above the riverbed, facing upstream with a natural swimming attitude. To increase the chances of catching a fish, a third fly can be tied on a top dropper so that it is suspended higher up in the water.

An indicator made from high-visibility monofilament, often with two different contrasting colours such as fluorescent red and yellow, is used to indicate takes. Whenever it stops moving, even for an instant, the angler should strike immediately because more than often a fish will have been hooked.

Fishing at close quarters in deeper water, use a Czech and Polish nymphing rig *(see page 47)*. For longer distance fishing in shallow water (where it is more likely that the fish will be spooked) the longer French style leaders are more likely to be successful.

In rough water Spanish leaders *(see page 47)* can be more effective at long distance.

Generally, lightweight, #2, 10 foot fly-rods are used for nymph fishing because it is easier to cast the light leaders with them.

A typical nymphing rig

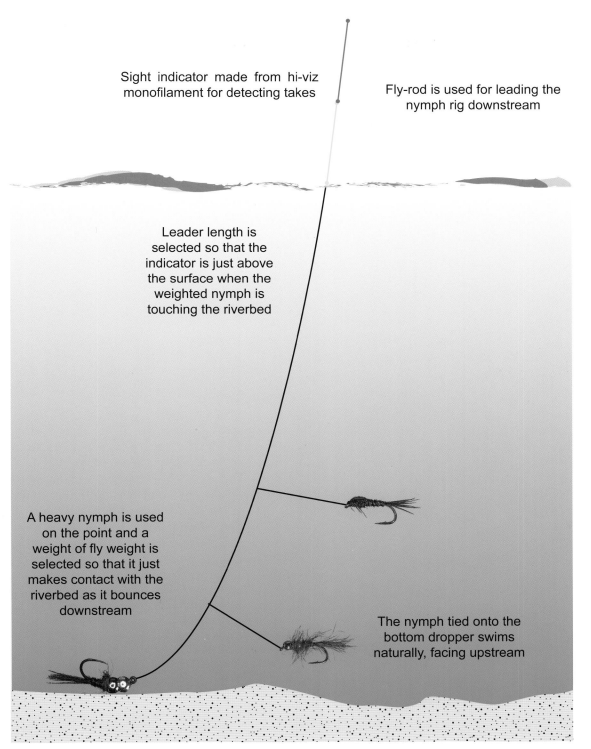

Sight indicator made from hi-viz monofilament for detecting takes

Fly-rod is used for leading the nymph rig downstream

Leader length is selected so that the indicator is just above the surface when the weighted nymph is touching the riverbed

A heavy nymph is used on the point and a weight of fly weight is selected so that it just makes contact with the riverbed as it bounces downstream

The nymph tied onto the bottom dropper swims naturally, facing upstream

Essential nymph patterns

Heavy Nymph
Hook: Size 10 jig hook
Thread: Black 8/0
Tail: Pheasant tail fibres
Rib: Fine copper wire
Body: Pheasant tail fibres
Thorax: Peacock glister dubbing
Head: 2 x 4mm tungsten beads

Pheasant Tail Nymph
Hook: Size 12 heavyweight down eye
Thread: Black 8/0
Tail: Pheasant tail fibres
Body: Pheasant tail fibres
Rib: Copper wire
Thorax: Pheasant tail fibres
Wing cover: Pheasant tail fibres

Gold-ribbed Hare's Ear
Hook: Size 12-14 heavyweight down eye
Thread: Brown or yellow 8/0
Tail: Hare's body hairs
Body: Dark hare's fur
Rib: Fine gold oval tinsel
Head: 3mm gold tungsten bead

Pink Shrimp
Hook: Size 10-12 heavyweight straight eye, wide gape
Thread: Pink 8/0
Rib: Clear monofilament nylon
Body: Pink seal's fur
Shell-back: Clear polythene strip

Tungsten-head pheasant tail nymph
Hook: Size 16 heavyweight down eye
Thread: Black 8/0
Tail: Pheasant tail fibres
Rib: Fine copper wire
Body: Pheasant tail fibres
Thorax: Peacock glister dubbing
Head: 2.5mm copper coated tungsten bead

Tungsten-head pheasant tail nymph
As above but with...
Head: 2.5mm bright orange painted tungsten bead

Leader lengths for nymphing

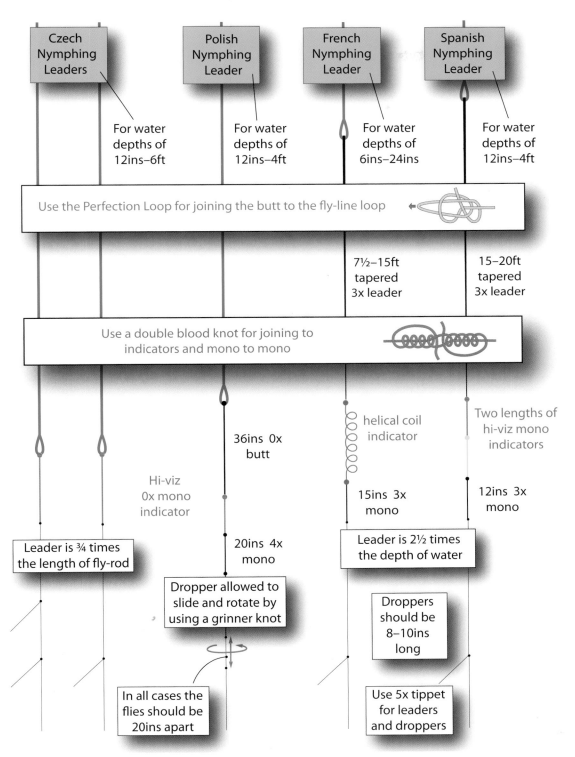

Czech Nymphing Leaders

Polish Nymphing Leader

French Nymphing Leader

Spanish Nymphing Leader

For water depths of 12ins–6ft

For water depths of 12ins–4ft

For water depths of 6ins–24ins

For water depths of 12ins–4ft

Use the Perfection Loop for joining the butt to the fly-line loop

7½–15ft tapered 3x leader

15–20ft tapered 3x leader

Use a double blood knot for joining to indicators and mono to mono

helical coil indicator

Two lengths of hi-viz mono indicators

36ins 0x butt

Hi-viz 0x mono indicator

15ins 3x mono

12ins 3x mono

20ins 4x mono

Leader is ¾ times the length of fly-rod

Leader is 2½ times the depth of water

Dropper allowed to slide and rotate by using a grinner knot

Droppers should be 8–10ins long

In all cases the flies should be 20ins apart

Use 5x tippet for leaders and droppers

Reading the river

As the flyfisher gains more experience with fishing rivers and streams, he or she develops the ability to 'read the water' and to predict where the fish are most likely to be feeding or hiding. By targeting these areas the prospect of catching a fish is greatly improved.

The diagram opposite depicts the features of a typical river and where there is a good chance that fish might be found.

1 Wherever there are large rocks it is likely that deep holes have been scoured out during flooding or high water. These are usually found to the side or behind the rocks and are a favourite position for trout and grayling to hold, because they feel protected and can easily intercept passing food. When a weighted nymph is guided alongside the rock and sunk deep it will often be taken by a fish.

2 The neck of a pool often attracts feeding fish because nymphs and other insects can become dislodged in the riffle above the pool and so the fish lie in wait for easy pickings.

3 Trees and bushes attract all sorts of terrestrial insects, and from time to time some will fall into the water. Fish are aware of this and will often take a fly the instant it hits the water, especially if it lands with a plop.

4 Fish like to lie in the deep water on a bend in the river, where the water has cut into the bank, making it high-sided. Often on the opposite side of the river there is a characteristic gravel bar. Fish feel safe in the deep water and food is constantly funnelled towards them because of the converging currents. Fishing the deep part of the pool with a team of nymphs will often result in hooking a fish.

5 Another good location for finding fish is the tail of the pool and often they will lie just in front of the lip of water before it runs into the next riffle. It is best to fish this from below the riffle, so that there is little disturbance of the water in the pool but sometimes the fish will take a dry or wet fly which is skated along the lip of the pool.

6 Riffle will often hold fish, even though the water is fairly shallow. They will lie in pockets of water behind stones fairly safe from predation and close to a food source, which is usually nymphs or caddis clinging to the stones. Sometimes grayling will actually burrow with their noses under the stones and flick them over to dislodge insects.

7 A classic place to find fish is in the crease of water that occurs between a fast flowing stretch and a back eddy. The fish can hold in this slack water without using too much energy and intercept food as it is channelled right past their noses by the fast-flowing current. The water here is often quite deep and this is usually one of the most productive spots in the whole river.

8 Some fish will sit in the back eddy itself because food is swept back round by the current and then presented slowly to the fish, where they are waiting. Note that the fish in this position are facing downstream and so the fly has to approach them from this direction.

9 Weed beds provide good shelter for fish and often they will dart out to intercept insects as they float past, either on or in the water. The weeds themselves provide a good habitat for insects.

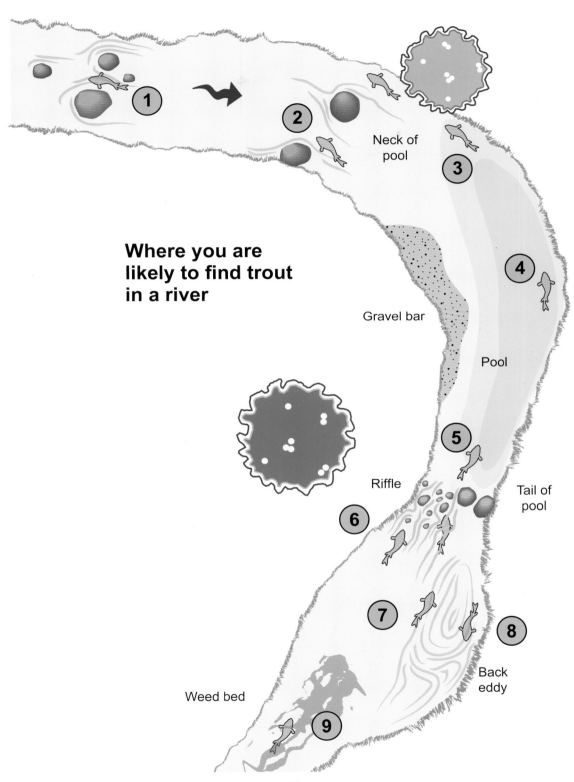

Where you are likely to find trout in a river

Neck of pool

Gravel bar

Pool

Riffle

Tail of pool

Back eddy

Weed bed

49

FISHING THE CADDIS IMITATION

A popular, recent addition to the sport of flyfishing is that of Czech nymphing, which has proved to be a successful way of catching trout and grayling in international river competitions. However, prior to its introduction, fishing a sedge pupa or dry sedge pattern, especially from a boat on reservoirs, was already a proven favourite of many anglers.

Stony riverbeds are a natural habitat for nymphs and caddis pupae. Turn over almost any stone and you will see a caddis case attached to it; sometimes a cluster of them. They exist in many sizes from micro caddis to almost an inch in length. Throughout the year, you can catch trout or grayling with one or a team of nymph patterns.

There are many familiar, traditional, fly patterns that mimic the sedge. Some of the better known are the Amber Sedge and Soldier Palmer which are pupa imitations, the Klinkhamer representing an emerging sedge and the Elk Hair Sedge, a very buoyant, dry fly.

Many types of flyfishing have evolved from imitating the characteristics of the caddis. There is nymphing, in various forms, reservoir and stillwater fishing, and dry fly fishing.

Caddisflies (Trichoptera)

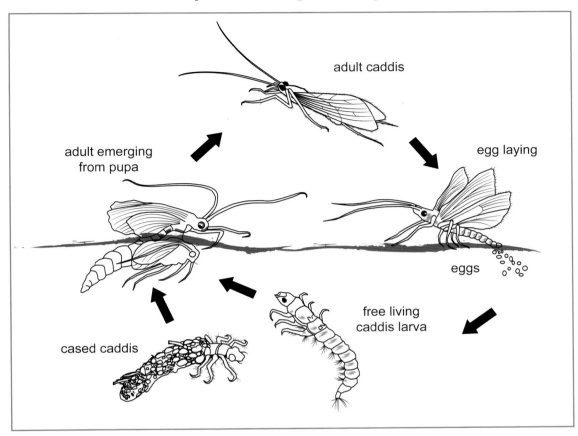

adult caddis

adult emerging from pupa

egg laying

eggs

free living caddis larva

cased caddis

Although it is not immediately apparent, caddis larvae are more prolific than mayfly nymphs in most rivers, streams and stillwaters. For this reason they are of considerable importance to the flyfisher, next only to the midge pupae.

The technique of Czech nymphing was based specifically on fishing with imitations of the Hydropsyche and Rhyacophilia caddis larvae.

Adult caddis (known sometimes as sedge) are often mistaken for moths, but they can be identified by the fine hairs on their wings, which are folded back over the body in a roof shape. They have long antennae and fly in swarms around the waterside.

The larvae exist in different forms. Some are free-swimming, and are usually found in running water or near to inlets feeding larger lakes, whilst others build cases from small pieces of grit, or from twigs and other debris. They can be found on the riverbed, attached to stones.

Their bodies are long and segmented with six legs located close to the head. When they are ready to pupate, the cased versions seal themselves in, whilst the free-swimming species build a cocoon from grit and other river bed materials. After pupation, which can last from a few days to two or three weeks, they emerge and swim to the surface, or towards the shore, where they climb up vegetation. Often when they are swimming they leave a tell-tale wake behind them which attracts feeding fish, which rise savagely to take them. This often occurs at the end of the day, near to dusk, and it is easy for the angler to mimic the natural, by skating the dry fly imitation, to great effect.

Essential caddis patterns

Klinkhamer
Hook: Size 10-16 grub hook
Thread: Black 8/0 uni-thread or similar
Tag: Glo brite #5
Body: Black flexi floss
Post: Tiemco aero dry fly wing
Thorax: Peacock glister
Hackle: Badger cock feather

Elk Hair Sedge
Hook: Medium weight down-eye 10-14
Thread: Brown 8/0 uni-thread or similar
Rib: Fine gold wire
Body: Green seal's fur
Wing: Natural elk's hair
Beard: Furnace cock hackle fibres

Czech Nymph
Hook: Barbless Czech nymph style
Thread: White uni nylon 70 denier or similar
Body: ⅓ light tan, ⅓ olive and ⅓ black synthetic dubbing
Inner Rib: Fine gold wire
Wing Cover: A strip of nymph skin, latex or other similar material

Making a sliding and rotating dropper

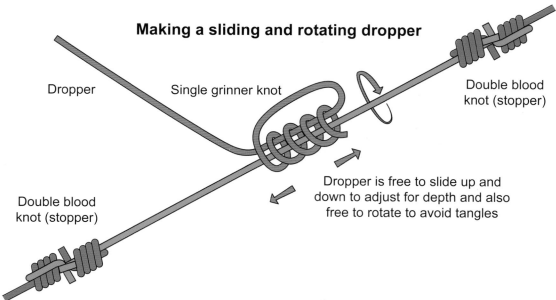

Dropper

Single grinner knot

Double blood knot (stopper)

Double blood knot (stopper)

Dropper is free to slide up and down to adjust for depth and also free to rotate to avoid tangles

New Zealand style

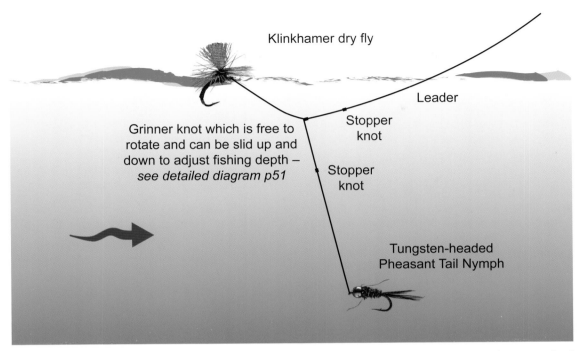

Klinkhamer dry fly

Leader

Grinner knot which is free to
rotate and can be slid up and
down to adjust fishing depth –
see detailed diagram p51

Stopper
knot

Stopper
knot

Tungsten-headed
Pheasant Tail Nymph

One of the best ways of fishing a nymph pattern at a controlled depth is by using the New Zealand style of fishing, depicted in the diagram above. The rig comprises a very buoyant and visible dry fly connected to a moveable dropper and a weighted nymph tied to the point of the leader.

The dry fly that has been chosen in this example is a Klinkhamer, with a brightly coloured wing post and a parachute hackle, which causes the fly to sit in the water surface, in a similar way to an emerging caddis fly. The weighted fly is a small, tungsten-headed, Pheasant Tail Nymph, which sinks quickly in the water and also pulls the dry fly down into the surface film. You will see that the nymph is swimming with a natural attitude, facing into the current.

The dropper is attached to the main leader with a grinner knot, allowing it to rotate freely and slide up and down. The freedom of movement of the dropper, along the leader, can be adjusted by tightening up the grinner. This arrangement allows the dropper to be repositioned so that the nymph swims at the required depth, depending on the speed of the current and height of the water level. The nymph can be fished just off the river bed or higher in the water depending on what the fish are feeding on at the time.

The dry fly acts as an indicator and whenever it stops drifting or dips in the water the angler should strike immediately because there is a good chance that a fish has taken the nymph. Occasionally a fish will rise and take the dry fly, in preference to the nymph.

A second dropper with an unweighted nymph can be tied on about 20ins (500mm) above the point fly to increase the odds of catching a fish.

This rig can be fished, effectively, at a distance and is normally cast up or across stream to minimise drag. The weighted nymph helps to achieve a good turnover and presentation. To maintain control, the rod-tip is lifted as the flies come close to the angler and then lowered as they pass on downstream. Providing the drift is drag-free it is worthwhile to continue fishing downstream, which will also make it easier to cast back upstream by using a tension cast.

FLY CASTING

The main reason why many beginners and even experienced flyfishers have problems with casting is because they have never understood the basic objectives.

The purpose of the cast is to use the fly-line to carry the fly and place it on the water where it is likely to attract a fish. For this to be achieved the fly-line must be airborne, turn over and roll out, straight, so that the fly lands delicately and accurately.

Every cast comprises at least one back cast and one forward cast but it can have more, usually depending on the length of line to be aerialised. The back cast positions the fly-line behind the rod-tip, as straight as possible, in the exact opposite direction to the forward cast. Once the fly-line is as straight as possible behind the angler [1] it is a relatively easy matter to push it forward to complete the cast [2] and [3].

To keep the fly-line straight it is important to:

*   Keep the fly-line under tension by continuously accelerating the rod-tip. If your rod merely moves at the same speed or if it slows down then tension and control of your fly-line will be lost.

*   Move the rod-tip in a *straight* aerial line, until you come to the abrupt stop [3].

These objectives may seem simple but the skill comes in moving the fly-rod with the correct acceleration to match the rod action and keeping the rod-tip on a very straight line.

The importance of maintaining a straight rod-tip path

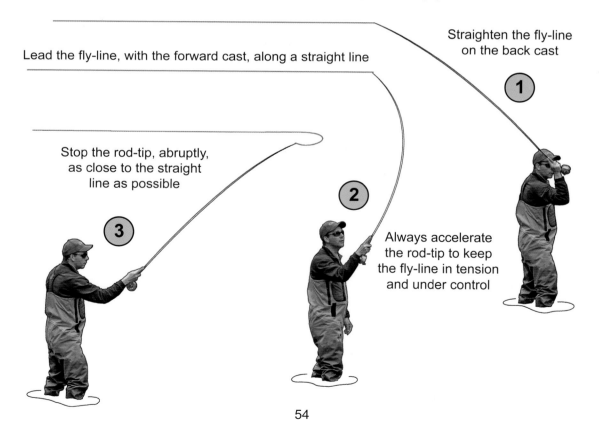

Straighten the fly-line on the back cast

Lead the fly-line, with the forward cast, along a straight line

1

Stop the rod-tip, abruptly, as close to the straight line as possible

2

3

Always accelerate the rod-tip to keep the fly-line in tension and under control

The roll cast

The roll cast is a simple one and particularly useful in confined spaces. It can be used when line has been stripped off the reel, to propel the fly-line out onto the water. It can be used for flicking the fly-line back upstream after fishing down, or for raising a sunk line up to the surface of the water before doing another cast. It may also be used for positioning the fly-line in preparation for lifting into a back cast, or at the end of every Spey cast prior to making the forward cast.

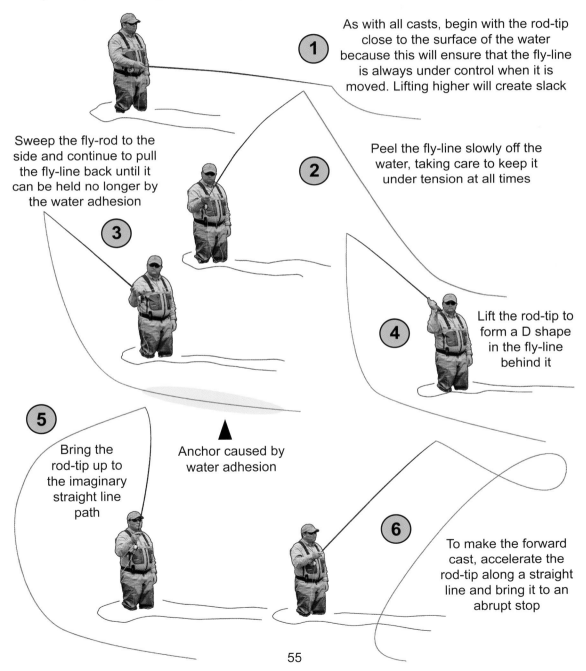

1 As with all casts, begin with the rod-tip close to the surface of the water because this will ensure that the fly-line is always under control when it is moved. Lifting higher will create slack

2 Peel the fly-line slowly off the water, taking care to keep it under tension at all times

Sweep the fly-rod to the side and continue to pull the fly-line back until it can be held no longer by the water adhesion

3

4 Lift the rod-tip to form a D shape in the fly-line behind it

5 Bring the rod-tip up to the imaginary straight line path

Anchor caused by water adhesion

6 To make the forward cast, accelerate the rod-tip along a straight line and bring it to an abrupt stop

More casting skills

Most flyfishers these days have their first angling experience on stillwaters. Overhead casting *(see page 56)* is the simplest method of getting the fly in front of the fish. It is not necessary to change the direction of the cast: just cast the fly-line out from the bankside and then retrieve the fly back.

Casting is a very big subject and this section is limited to two essential styles. There is also a short description of the straight line path *(see page 54)*, which is probably the most important concept in casting, even though this is not widely appreciated. In practice it is difficult to achieve a completely straight line path and so at best it is a compromise.

Our ability to change casting direction (with both the roll cast and the overhead cast) is very limited for the simple reason that the fly-line cannot be straightened easily at another angle, during the back cast or forward cast. Also, the overhead cast requires a lot of clearance behind the caster for the back cast to fully extend. It is for this reason that Spey casting *(photo below)* was developed – to enable the angler to change the casting angle in a restricted space, and with different wind conditions – a skill that is well worth learning if you wish to advance in to river fishing.

For more detailed explanations of all types of casting techniques, with both single- and two-handed fly rods, you may like to read the companion book to this one: *Flycasting Skills* by John Symonds.

It is available direct from the publisher Merlin Unwin Books or from all major booksellers and tackle shops.

ISBN 978-1-906122-49-2

The book uses easy-to-follow diagrams, similar to the ones in this section on casting. Step-by-step instructions take you through the stages of each cast with helpful tips and fault-finding information. It also covers choice of tackle.

FLYCASTING SKILLS

for beginner and expert

John Symonds & Philip Maher

• Overhead cast • Roll cast • Spey cast • Jump Roll
• Snap-T cast • Snake Roll • Galway cast • Skagit cast
• Underhand cast • Double hauling • Loops & anchors
• all the Single- and Double-handed variations
• plus great advice on rods, reels and flylines

The lift and overhead cast

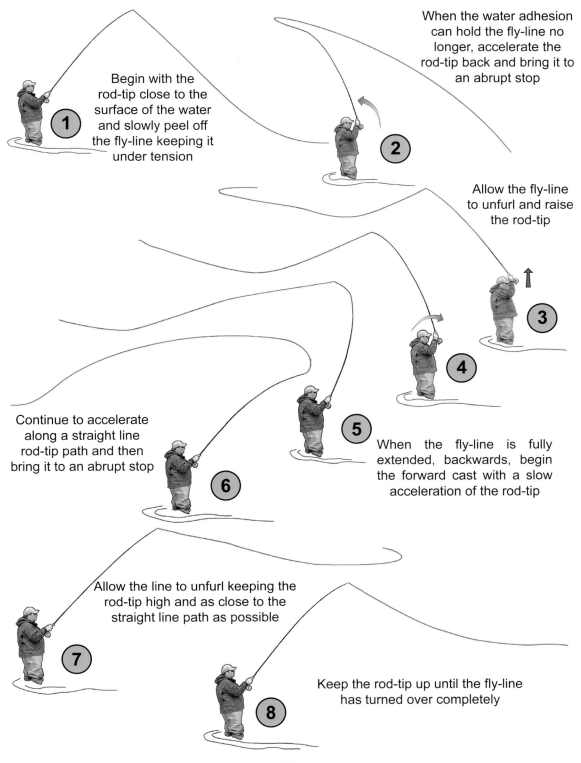

Begin with the rod-tip close to the surface of the water and slowly peel off the fly-line keeping it under tension

When the water adhesion can hold the fly-line no longer, accelerate the rod-tip back and bring it to an abrupt stop

Allow the fly-line to unfurl and raise the rod-tip

When the fly-line is fully extended, backwards, begin the forward cast with a slow acceleration of the rod-tip

Continue to accelerate along a straight line rod-tip path and then bring it to an abrupt stop

Allow the line to unfurl keeping the rod-tip high and as close to the straight line path as possible

Keep the rod-tip up until the fly-line has turned over completely

Drag-free drift

It is essential to mimic the movement of the natural insect in the water, especially when fishing rivers. This applies not only when your fly is on the surface but also below it and this is often overlooked. Water close to the river bed always flows slower than the surface layer and so sunk nymphs must be fished at a more gradual pace than that indicated by objects on the surface.

The use of a very fine tippet, connected to the end of a tapered leader, can help with deception because it lands in a series of slack loops, allowing the fly to float freely (referred to as 'dead drift').

The causes of drag

Casting across the stream at a right angle will inevitably result in a belly in the fly-line (faster mid-stream flow) which will drag the fly at an unnatural speed, usually resulting in it being ignored by fish *(see diagram below)*. On rare occasions, skating the fly across the surface may entice a fish to take if this is what some natural insects (such as sedges) are doing.

The causes of drag

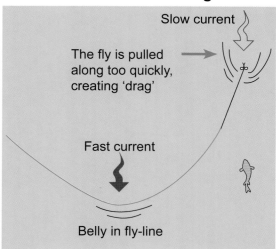

Slow current

The fly is pulled along too quickly, creating 'drag'

Fast current

Belly in fly-line

Casting to avoid drag

However, in most instances, it is much better to cast upstream above the fish *(see opposite)* enabling the fly-line and the fly to drift back at the same speed, without any drag. Furthermore, fish usually face upstream into the current so they are less likely to be spooked. Whilst the fly is floating downstream, the fly-line can be retrieved and held in coils so that tension is maintained. The coils can be released back into the aerialised line during the next cast (this is referred to as 'shooting line'). The strategy is to gradually work upstream, repeating this process.

The aim is to drop the fly a few feet upstream of the fish so that it has time to see and intercept it. So, where possible, cast up and across the stream so that the fish have less chance of seeing the fly-line or leader.

Once the fly has landed in the water, leave it there, allowing the current to drift it naturally over the fish. Any fly-line manipulation to reduce the drag should be carried out during the cast, in the air *(see 'upstream mend' opposite)*. This is referred to as 'mending the line' and often involves a very simple 'flip' of the fly-rod during the aerial forward cast, before the fly-line drops on the water. The objective is to place a bend in the fly-line where the fastest current is and so this allows time for the fly to swim without drag before the fly-line bellies and starts pulling the fly along at an unnatural speed.

When casting downstream, the drag-free drift can be induced by generating a series of wiggles in the fly-line, which will straighten whilst the fly-line is floating downstream *(see 'wiggle cast' opposite)*.

Methods of presenting the fly

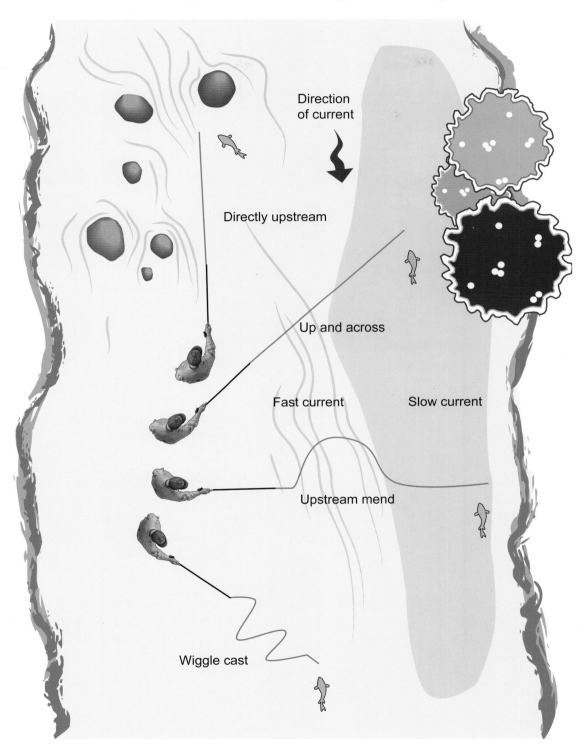

Direction of current

Directly upstream

Up and across

Fast current

Slow current

Upstream mend

Wiggle cast

TENKARA

Archaeological evidence shows the use of bamboo rods and artificial lures in Japan as early as the 9th century BC, but the first written evidence dates to the 17th century AD. Recently, Tenkara has become a very popular fishing method, worldwide. The word Tenkara means 'from heaven', which could describe the way in which the fly (kebari) is presented.

It has a lot of appeal to the beginner because of its simplicity, the tackle is inexpensive and light and it is a very effective way of catching trout and grayling, providing they are not too large.

By using a long rod and leader (a conventional fly-line and reel is not required) it is possible to fish, with no drag, by suspending the fly in or below the surface of the water and to create animation by movement of the rod-tip, which has the result of attracting fish.

The original rods were made from bamboo but the modern equivalents, which are made from carbon fibre are typically 11-15ft long, telescopic and very flexible. This means that they are lightweight and portable. Straight monofilament can be used for connecting the fly to the rod-tip.

Basic Tackle Requirements

- ☐ 13ft Tenkara rod with a 6:4 soft action
- ☐ Pair of line keepers *(see picture opposite)*
- ☐ Spool of hi-viz fluorocarbon or copolymer leader – 0.35mm diameter
- ☐ Bite indicator made from braid or straight monofilament
- ☐ (Optional) A furled leader
- ☐ (Optional) A tapered leader
- ☐ 6x (3lb breaking strength) copolymer tippet
- ☐ Fly box with compartments and slotted foam
- ☐ Forceps
- ☐ Line snips
- ☐ A long-handled landing net
- ☐ Waders
- ☐ Fishing hat or baseball cap
- ☐ Polaroid glasses

Tenkara rods

Tenkara rods: note the clips, the 'keepers', for storing the line.

Rods supplied by Tenkara Centre UK.

Compared with the Western equivalents, modern Tenkara tackle is much simpler but just as effective for catching fish (although most fans would argue that it is even better). Nevertheless, there are skills that need to be developed when fishing Tenkara-style, for instance the method of casting and presenting the fly with very light lines.

Certainly the Tenkara system allows the angler to present the fly delicately, and to fish it with very little drag, even in rough pockets of water. There is no fly-reel and fly-line and the leader is connected directly to the rod-tip. What this means is that the fly can be manipulated as it is drifting, to simulate the action of a living insect, which of course will attract fish. Furthermore, the fly can be guided accurately over the more productive runs of water.

It is a stealthier way of fishing because Tenkara rods are long, enabling the angler to fish at a distance with no fly-line resting on the water, visible to the fish. Therefore fish are less likely to be spooked.

It is possible to fish with straight monofilament, which is inexpensive and can be cut to any length depending on the prevailing conditions such as the depth of water. The use of a hi-viz leader might be beneficial for observing and developing casting technique. For better turnover and gentler presentation, a furled leader can be used instead of monofilament but these are more expensive. Alternatively, hand-tied tapered leaders are favoured by some Tenkara fishers.

When they are not in use, Tenkara rods can be retracted to a very compact and convenient length, due to their telescopic design. This makes them very easy to carry in a small back pack. For convenience the leader can be wrapped around simple 'keepers' _(see above)_, attached to the rod with 'O' rings, for instant use and to prevent tangling.

The action of a Tenkara rod is determined by the ratio of stiff butt length to flexible tip length, such as 5:5 (soft action), 6:4 or 7:3 (tip action).

Rod-tips are prone to breakage through careless handling whilst attaching the line or whilst freeing stuck line but are not difficult or expensive to replace.

Typical Tenkara rigs

The reason why Tenkara fishing is so successful is because the fly-line is kept *off* the water and this is achieved by using relatively short, light lines. Tenkara lines can be constructed from high-visibility monofilament but modern fluorocarbon level lines are the most popular. A few people use copolymer level lines, tapered copolymer or fluorocarbon lines or furled lines, which give a better turnover of the fly. Fluorocarbon is much thinner and easier to hold off the water but it is prone to sinking and so requires a coating of floatant, which has to be frequently replenished. However, fluorocarbon is not biodegradable, whereas copolymers are.

It is easier to land fish with a shorter line, when using the Tenkara technique, bearing in mind the limitations imposed by the strength of the rod-tip, because this makes hand-lining easier. It is advisable to have a line and tippet combined length which is no longer than 1ft more than the rod length.

A typical dry fly set-up comprises a level line that is between 1-3ft shorter than the Tenkara rod length and a tippet which is between 2-3ft long. A mini perfection loop can be tied into the end of the line for connecting the tippet by means of a blood knot *(see page 18)*.

The rod is held out and high to fish the dry fly on the surface of the water with no drag. The fly should land on the water first, followed by the minimum amount of tippet.

The nymphing (bugging) configuration uses a shorter line, say about 5ft shorter than the length of the rod, with approximately 5ft of tippet. The two are joined together with a brightly coloured indicator (approximately 6in long), looped at both ends for a blood knot connection. The nymph is cast upstream and led back downstream from the rod-tip and ideally it should be bouncing along the riverbed.

The line is connected to the rod by means of a short length of braid, called a *lilian*, which slips over and is glued onto the rod-tip.

Connecting the line to the lilian

The knot connection of the line to the lilian is fairly simple to tie and to release, when the line is changed. The diagram below shows how this is done. For clarity the lilian is depicted in red and the line is coloured blue.

1 First of all take the end of the fly-line and tie an **overhand knot** in it. This will prevent the main knot from slipping under tension.

2 Next make a loop and pass the tag end around the base of the loop, securing it with a **thumb knot** (like tying a shoe-lace).

3 Now tie an overhand knot in the tag end of the **lilian** to prevent this from slipping through the slip-knot tied in the fly-line, when it is pulled tight.

4 Pass the tag end of the lilian through the line loop twice and pull the loop down on the lilian.

You will now have a simple knot which can be released quickly by pulling the tag ends of the line and the lilian in opposite directions to each other.

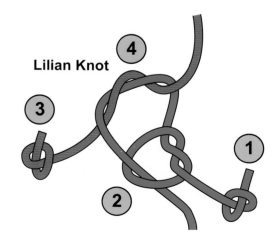

Lilian Knot

The Tenkara set-up

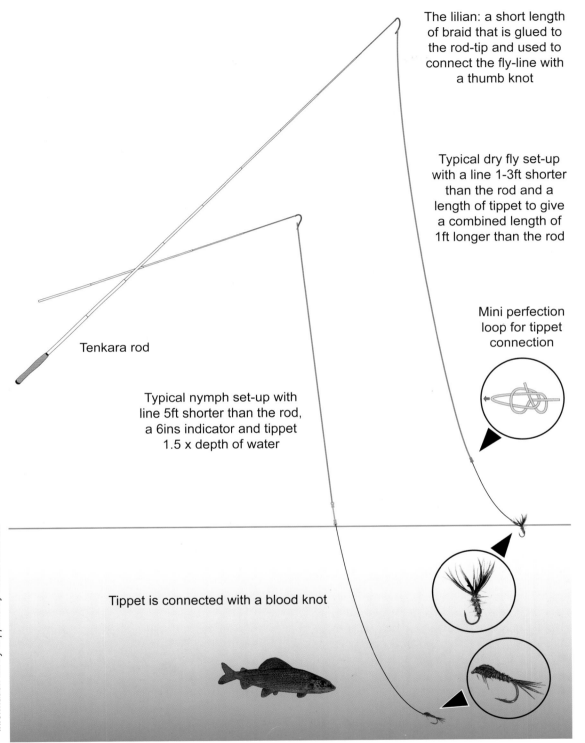

The lilian: a short length of braid that is glued to the rod-tip and used to connect the fly-line with a thumb knot

Typical dry fly set-up with a line 1-3ft shorter than the rod and a length of tippet to give a combined length of 1ft longer than the rod

Mini perfection loop for tippet connection

Tenkara rod

Typical nymph set-up with line 5ft shorter than the rod, a 6ins indicator and tippet 1.5 x depth of water

Tippet is connected with a blood knot

Information kindly supplied by David Southall

Essential Tenkara fly patterns

Grey Sakasa Kebari
Hook: Size 14 or 12 barbless
Thread: Grey
Hackle: Grey/white grizzle hen, tied reversed
Body: Dubbed grey hare's fur
Rib: White 6/0 thread

Royal Coachman Sakasa Kebari
Hook: Size 14 or 12 barbless
Thread: Red
Hackle: Medium red hen, tied reversed
Body: Peacock herl with red floss silk centre

Ishigaki Kebari
Hook: Size 14 or 12 barbless
Thread: Black
Hackle: Grizzle hen, dyed olive, tied reversed
Body: Black tying silk, tapered to thorax

Gold-Ribbed Hare's Ear
Hook: Size 14 or 12 barbless
Thread: Beige
Hackle: Hen pheasant back, or Partridge back – tied reversed
Body: Natural hare's fur
Rib: Fine gold tinsel

Flies tied by Louis Noble

Finding the fish Tenkara-style

Virtually any Western-style fly can be fished with Tenkara tackle. This includes dry and wet flies, unweighted and weighted nymphs and streamers. In the main the Tenkara flies, or 'Kebari' as they are called, are sparsely tied, have reversed, soft hackles as shown in the selection of trout flies on the opposite page, some of which have been adopted from Western patterns. Like the tackle, the best patterns are simple.

Skilled Tenkara fishers will fish with just one pattern and because the technique is so versatile they can use the same fly as a substitute for dry, emerger, wet and nymph patterns simply by the way that they control the fly in the water.

The flies can be fished in very fast riffles by keeping all but the very end of the tippet off the water, allowing the fly to drift downstream and lifting slowly at the end of the drift.

Eddies are easy to fish with a Tenkara set-up because there is no line on the water to hinder the drift. Eddies are often overlooked by anglers fishing Western-style but they often hold fish.

Pocket water is difficult to fish using conventional techniques, but with Tenkara the fly can be allowed to drown in the water as it flows into the mini pool, and it sinks to the bottom, taken down by the swirling currents.

In pools the fly can be fished as a nymph. Start by sinking the fly and then, beginning at the tail of the pool, methodically work upstream, covering the far bank (if it is within reach) and then fishing the bottom of the riffle at the head of the pool.

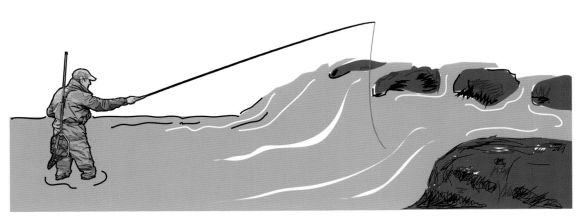

Fishing pocket water using the Tenkara system

SALMON FISHING

When salmon return from the sea to spawn in freshwater, they no longer feed and so it is a mystery why they take a fly. It could be an instinctive reflex, from their days as parr when they had voracious appetites, or maybe they are just being curious or aggressive – no one really knows the reason.

Movement and shape appear to be the most important characteristics of a salmon fly, followed by colour and size but there is no obvious logical approach to selecting a suitable fly pattern. Often it is just a question of using whatever has been successful or is popular on the river in question or perhaps a particular favourite which can be fished with confidence.

The clarity of the water is also significant and for this reason, in peat-coloured rivers a dark claret fly might be successful. Orange and yellow are also popular colours, when the river is brown, and black when it is clear. A mixture of these three colours can be used for general-purpose flies.

Basic Tackle Requirements

- ☐ #10 15ft fly-rod
- ☐ #10 Spey line with tips of different sinking rates
- ☐ #10 fly-reel
- ☐ 12ft 15lb breaking strength, nylon tapered leader for salmon fishing
- ☐ Spools of 14lb and 12lb leader
- ☐ Salmon fly-box
- ☐ Forceps
- ☐ Line snips
- ☐ Landing net
- ☐ Polaroid glasses
- ☐ Waders
- ☐ Wading staff
- ☐ Wading jacket
- ☐ Fishing hat or baseball cap

Essential salmon patterns

Cascade
Hook: Double size 10 or 12
Thread: 8/0 Black uni-thread
Tail: Mixed orange and yellow bucktail with four strands of pearly crystal hair
Body: Back silver mylar; front black floss
Rib: Medium oval silver tinsel
Wing: Black squirrel hair with pearl crystal hair
Hackles: Yellow and orange cock

Willy Gunn (Tube Fly)
Hook: Tube fly treble
Thread: 8/0 Black uni-thread
Body: Black floss
Rib: Medium oval silver tinsel
Wing: Mixed orange, yellow and black bucktail

Silver Stoat
Hook: Double size 12 or 14
Thread: 8/0 Black uni-thread
Tail: Golden pheasant topping
Body: Silver mylar
Rib: Small oval silver tinsel
Wing: Black squirrel hair
Beard: Black cock hackle

Pot Belly Pig
Hook: Tube fly hook
Thread: Red
Tail: 4-6 orange-dyed boar bristles, orange bucktail and 3-4 strands of pearl tinsel
Rear hackle: Dyed orange cock
Body: Orange Antron
Body hackle: Black cock
Rib: Oval gold tinsel
Cheeks: Jungle cock

Collie Dog
Hook: Tube fly hook
Thread: Black
Body: Plastic tube
Wing: Black goat hair
Hackle: Red cock

Flies tied by Alberto Laidlaw

Locating salmon in rivers

Many salmon anglers have fished the same stretches of water for a number of years and have built up a knowledge of where salmon are most likely to stop on their journey up the river. They will tend to focus their efforts around these areas and so increase their chances of catching a fish. The positions can change depending on the height and temperature of the water.

Without this knowledge or advice from the ghillie, it is up to you, the salmon angler, to read the water and decide where the salmon are most likely to be lying. The diagram on the opposite page illustrates the features in the river that are preferred by salmon, which are seeking safety from predation, well-oxygenated water and the minimum use of energy reserves.

(1) Salmon will often lie off the end of a croy (a stone platform built out into the river to help the angler to cover productive stretches of water). There is a temptation to walk up to the end of the croy and start fishing from there but this should be resisted because there is a good chance that any salmon resting there will be spooked. It is far better to cast from the back of the croy and allow the fly to dangle off the front of it. Better still, if it is possible, wade upstream of the croy and allow the fly to swing into it.

(2) Another good position is alongside, or in front of, large submerged rocks. These slow down the current by producing drag and so the salmon uses less energy and feels protected.

(3) When the weather is warm, the salmon will seek comfort in the deeper parts of the pool, often under the bank, where there is a bend in the river. Usually the water is quite shallow off the opposite bank and easy to wade.

(4) At the top of a stretch of turbulent, fast water a salmon often can be found resting just above the run, at the lip of the pool, tucked into the bank or just in front of any rocks that might be there. The flow of water can still be fairly rapid at this point but the fish seem to like this because it is easy to take oxygen through their gills, with very little effort.

(5) At the bottom of a run, the fish can sense the water pressure and will hold there until they are confident that they can move on upstream.

Covering the water

The water should be fished in a methodical manner, by casting at 45 degrees and allowing the fly to swing round at a pace that is similar to that of the current. Care should be taken to ensure that the belly of the fly-line does not pull the fly round at an unnatural speed because this is unlikely to attract salmon. Sometimes, however, if the current is very slow in a pool the angler may decide to cast at 90 degrees or put a downstream mend into the fly-line to increase the speed at which the fly travels. This may be accompanied by some movement of the fly induced by retrieving the fly-line.

The fly should travel in front of the identified taking spots and not be lifted out of the water too quickly at the end of the swing. Quite often a salmon will follow the fly around and take it when it stops or when it moves suddenly as it is lifted out of the water. To cover the water systematically, the angler makes one or two casts and then takes a step downstream, before repeating the process.

Except when the water is very low, it is quite common practice for the fly to be fished with a sink tip (intermediate or fast sinking rate) and a long leader (9-12ft) off a floating fly-line. Large tube flies are often used at the beginning of the season, or when river levels are high. As the water temperature rises, the flies become progressively smaller until, in high summer, size fourteen doubles may be the catching size.

As for colour, my preferred practice is to give the fly a swim in the water and look at it. If it appears to be too bright then change it for something that has a more subdued colour, similar to the natural prey that salmon feed on at sea.

Salmon lies

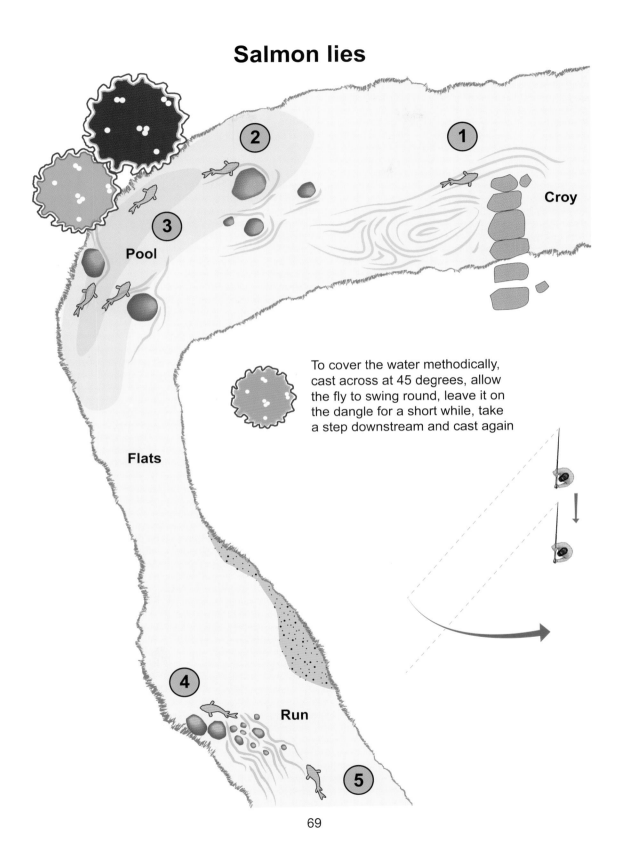

To cover the water methodically, cast across at 45 degrees, allow the fly to swing round, leave it on the dangle for a short while, take a step downstream and cast again

Croy

Pool

Flats

Run

Salmon fishing styles

Traditionally the salmon fisher has used long-bellied Spey lines which can be between 50ft and 80ft long. These were required to cover the wide salmon rivers. However with the advent of modern materials and lighter tackle, other techniques have evolved which make salmon fishing easier to perform, even in difficult conditions. This has also opened up the sport to the wider public because the basic casting skills can be learnt relatively quickly.

A **floating line** is generally not the first choice, unless the river level is low, in which case a long leader and a small fly would be employed, or when a surface lure is used, such as a hitched fly, which can be very successful on some rivers, particularly in Canada and Iceland. More likely it is necessary to use a sinking line of some description and there are **long-bellied Spey lines** with varying sink rates available. However it is not very practical for the salmon fisher to buy and carry lots of reels or spools with different lines on them, especially if different line weights are also needed.

To overcome this problem, **multi-tip Spey lines** were introduced by the tackle manufacturers and these comprise a floating belly section with a detachable front section with a loop-to-loop connection. This enables the angler to change the sink rate of the tip very quickly and to adapt to the desired fishing depth, depending on the time of season, water level and the force of the current. Tip lengths are generally 10ft or 15ft long and with some systems it is possible to join two tips together, to get a longer sinking section.

When there is a problem with limited back space for casting, then **shooting-heads** provide a good solution. The heads are relatively short; about 40ft long and are connected to the reel with a separate running line. If there is a large welded loop on the end of the running line *(see page 76)* it is easy to change shooting heads without uncoiling them, by passing the loop through the back loop on the fly-line, slipping it over the fly-reel and then pulling the loops together.

Shooting heads can have different sink rates but in addition a **poly-tip** with a smaller diameter and faster sink-rate can be attached to the front end of the line. These are normally between 10ft and 15ft long but very long poly leaders are also sometimes used to create a good anchor for the D-loop.

One of the easiest salmon fly-lines to use is the **Skagit line**, which was developed for lifting heavy flies and sink tips with relative ease, even for the unskilled caster. The main feature of the Skagit line is its large diameter, compact length and mass and buoyancy. The Skagit line is also used with a running line, which means that there is a fair amount of line that requires retrieving after the fly has been fished round to the dangle. Therefore a certain amount of line management is required, unlike with the long-bellied line. Some may consider this to be a disadvantage but others see it as a very effective way of inducing the salmon to take the fly.

The Skagit line is used in conjunction with a range of sink tips, normally 10ft or 12ft long with a section that has been impregnated with titanium dust to cause the front end of the tip to sink in a controlled manner (see MOW tips in diagram opposite – the dark brown indicates sinking portion).

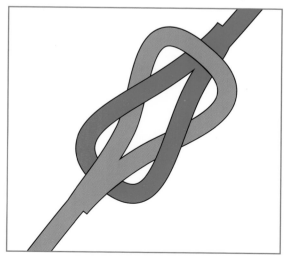

Loop-to-loop connection (for attaching different front sections to the fly-line)

Salmon fly-line options

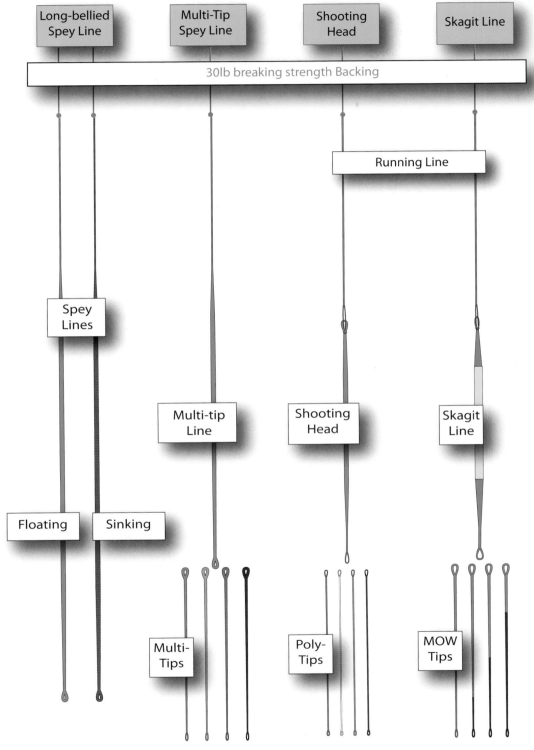

Long-bellied Spey Line

Multi-Tip Spey Line

Shooting Head

Skagit Line

30lb breaking strength Backing

Running Line

Spey Lines

Multi-tip Line

Shooting Head

Skagit Line

Floating

Sinking

Multi-Tips

Poly-Tips

MOW Tips

Double Turle Knot (salmon fly to leader)

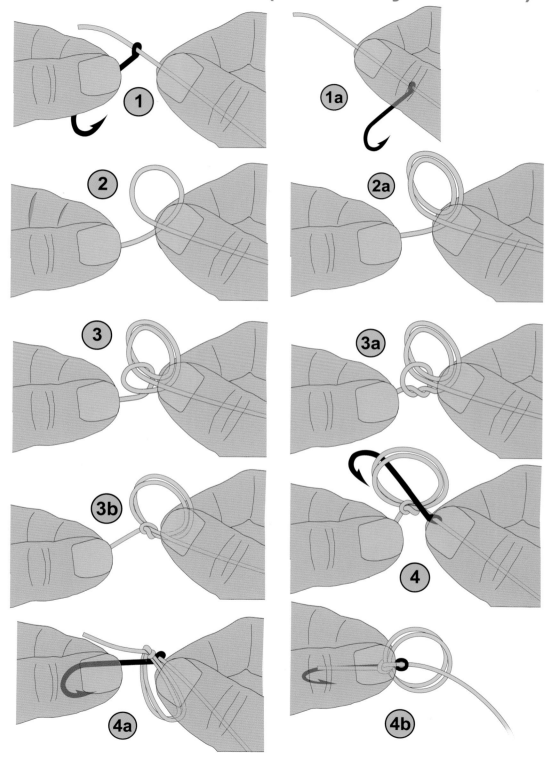

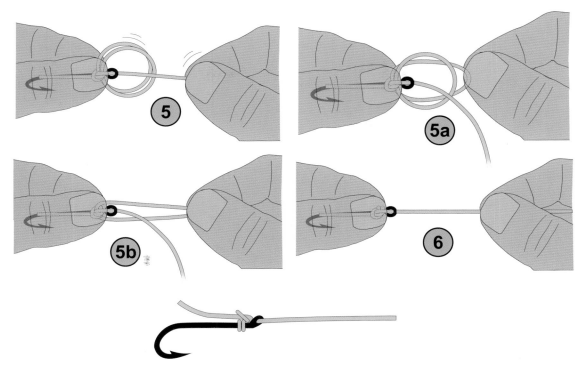

The double turle knot is used for connecting salmon flies to a leader. It allows the fly to swim in line with the leader. It is also a strong knot and allows free movement of the fly.

1 Begin by tying the leader onto the fly-line and then threading the tag end of the leader through the eye of the hook. Allow the hook to run down the leader.

2 Make two loops in the end of the leader, with one on top of the other.

3 Now tie the two loops together using a simple overhand knot. Pull the overhand knot tight.

4 Bring the hook back up the leader and pass the hook through the double loop. Hold the two loops and overhand knot together just behind the eye of the hook, between the thumb and forefinger.

5 Pull the leader and observe which of the two loops moves. Grasp hold of this moving loop and pull it, causing the other loop to close down on the hook shank.

6 Now pull the leader so that the other loop pulls down onto the hook shank. Check the loops to make sure that they are sitting together snugly and side by side.

Pull the leader hard to set the knot, whilst holding the tag end along the hook shank with the thumb and finger. The tag end should lie along the shank if the knot is tied correctly.

The double turle knot

73

Shooting heads

New methods of flyfishing for salmon are constantly evolving, just like all other branches of the sport and this is one of its attractions. There is always something new to learn and try. The introduction of lighter and more efficient tackle has opened up great possibilities and ingenious solutions.

One of the methods introduced by the Scandinavians, for use on rivers where there are back-casting limitations, is the use of shooting heads. Basically, these are short lines (approximately 40ft long for salmon fishing) that are attached to a running line with a loop-to-loop connection. The lines are easy to change over so different sink rates can be selected for changing river conditions. For convenience several lines can be coiled up and transported in a wallet. This avoids the need for several reel spools.

Shooting heads are designed with different front tapers to suit the preferred presentation method and the size/weight of the fly that is fished. For instance a heavy fly, such as a 3-inch brass tube, requires a fast taper for good turnover.

In addition to the shooting head it is possible to attach a poly-tip leader on the front end, which is also joined by using a loop-to-loop method. These can also have different sink rates and so different shooting head/tip combinations can be used for getting the fly to the desired depth.

A fly-rod with a fast tip-action is ideal with shooting heads (approximately 40ft long) which require only a short casting stroke. The underhand technique is used to create a fast rod-tip movement, reducing the need for much space for the back-cast. Underhand refers to the bottom hand, on a two-handed rod, which is used to accelerate the fly-line speed during the cast.

Skagit lines

The surge of recent interest in Skagit lines is because they simplify casting, particularly with sinking lines and heavy flies. They were developed in the North-West Pacific Coast rivers, primarily for fishing steelheads (large sea-going trout).

A Skagit line also has a short head that is connected to a running line but it is thicker than other lines and is very buoyant. Consequently the Skagit line can be placed on the water and allowed to 'set' (settle in the surface of the water). By peeling the line off the water's surface and then continuing to form a D-loop, it is possible to use the mass of the Skagit line and water resistance to lift sink tips and heavy flies with relative ease.

To cast the Skagit line it is necessary to use a short, two-handed fly-rod – up to 13ft long. A slower tip-to-middle action may also work well because there is a pause between moving the rod-tip and lifting the line off the water.

The Skagit line is always used with a tip attached to its front end (using a loop-to-loop connection). The tips range from floating to fast sinking. Additionally, the back end of the tip might be floating and the front end sinking in varying proportions: 5ft/5ft for example.

Because the shooting heads and Skagit lines are connected to a running line, it is important to develop the skills of line management, which are required to enable 'shooting' – in which the head pulls the running line out through the rings and enables long casts to be made.

This involves collecting the line in loops during retrieval and holding them with a finger, or fingers, for release after the fly-rod is stopped at the end of the forward casting stroke. Not only do the loops help to prevent tangles in the relatively thin running line but it also keeps the running line off the water.

Some casters, particularly Scandinavians, like to leave the running line on the water because this provides a certain amount of resistance during the forward cast which helps with a good turnover and presentation of the fly.

To cast a shooting head or Skagit line there must only be a short length of running line outside the rod-tip (known as 'overhang'). Therefore the running line has to be retrieved before the next cast can be made. This may be considered a drawback, compared with the long-bellied Spey lines which require very little line to be retrieved. However, the action of retrieving creates movement in the fly and this may well entice a salmon to take.

One final thought regarding the pros and cons of shooting heads and Skagit versus traditional Spey lines: the action of stripping line back, or retrieving, will draw more water through the rod rings and so in cold weather they will be more likely to ice up.

More detailed information on casting, line specifications and line management can be found in the companion book to this one, *Flycasting Skills (see page 56)*.

Clockwise from top left: wallet containing a range of MOW tips; a coiled MOW tip; yellow Skagit line connected to a large loop of running line coming off the reel; a MOW tip connected to the front of the Skagit line

How to make a Welded Loop

Most shooting heads are joined to the running line (and line-tips and poly-tips to their parent line) by using a loop-to-loop connection so that removal and changeover is both quick and easy.

Most modern fly-lines can be welded but the older PVC lines have a higher melting temperature and for this reason they cannot be welded.

(1) To prepare the fly-line, cut the end at an acute angle with a pair of sharp scissors, making the taper as long as possible to produce a smooth joint.

(2) Take a length of shrink-tube, approximately 1 inch (25mm) long and with a diameter just large enough to allow the shrink-tube to be pulled over a length of fly-line that has been doubled over on itself. Insert a length of monofilament through the shrink-tube and return the end back through the tube to make a loop.

(3) Insert the end of the fly-line through the loop of monofilament.

(4) Hold the shrink-tube in one hand and with the other hand pull the ends of the monofilament so that the loop closes down on the fly-line.

(5) Continue to pull the fly-line into the shrink-tube so that a loop of line is formed and the tapered section is trapped against the straight section in the centre of the shrink-tube.

(6) Using a gas cigarette lighter, slowly warm the loop joint that is contained within the shrink-tube. It is important that the welding process is started at one end of the shrink-tube and that the flame is gradually moved to the other end, so that no air is trapped within the joint, otherwise this will cause a bubble to form in the shrink-tube and spoil the joint.

(7) When the fly-line has melted and it can be seen that the joint has fused together, the joint can be made neater and stronger by rolling it on a flat surface with a lollipop stick or spoon handle, whilst the joint cools and re-hardens.

(8) Finally, the shrink-tube is removed by putting the point of a pair of scissors under one end and gradually snipping along the complete length of the shrink-tube.

With thin fly-lines, or those containing tungsten powder for fast-sinking properties, the shrink-tube may be left in situ, to provide extra strength.

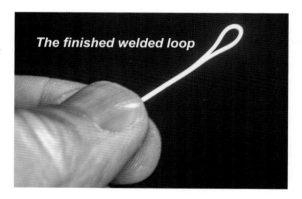

The finished welded loop

The beautiful simplicity of the Loop-to-Loop connection

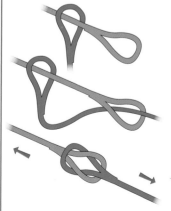

The loop of the line, or tippet, *(blue)* is slipped over the end of the parent line *(green)*

The flying end *(blue)* is passed through the loop of the parent line

The two lines are pulled apart to set the loop-to-loop connection

Welded Loop

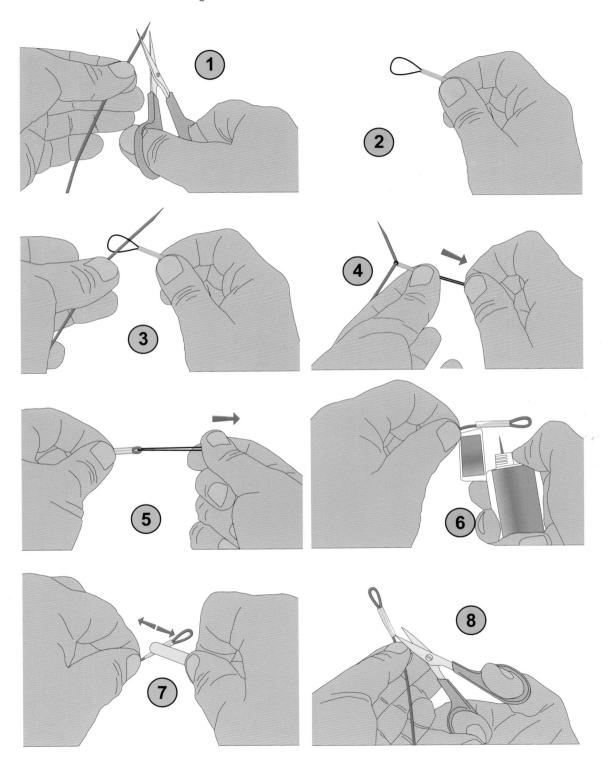

LEADERS

Leaders are the link between fly and fly-line. They are normally tapered with three distinct sections: the butt, taper and tippet. They can be any length from 1ft to 20ft or more.

The dimensions, material, density and length of the leader determine its function. For instance:

Type of leader	Function
Long butt section and short tippet	Delivers more energy to the fly, so is useful for accurate casting.
Fast taper with a short tippet and constructed from a stiff material	Provide faster turnover of the fly and so are used with bulkier flies or windy conditions.
Slow taper with a long tippet and constructed from a soft material	Selected to create slack when the fly is delivered to the water, thereby creating a drag-free drift.
Short, same-thickness length of nylon	Used with a sunken line to ensure that the fly is kept low in the water and is not pulled up by the current.
Furled leaders	For delicate presentation.
Poly-coated leaders	Available in different densities and selected for fishing the fly at a particular depth.
Length of nylon with droppers	For fishing a team of flies.
Bioabsorbal polymer	Biodegrades in 5 years.

Material	Characteristics
Nylon monofilament	Tends to absorb water (up to 20% of its own weight), which causes diameter to increase and breaking strength to decrease by about 20%.
Cofilaments (one nylon type sheathed over another nylon type)	
Copolymers (nylons chemically bonded to form larger polymers)	Is more buoyant, especially when greased, hence making it more suitable for dry flies.
	Specific gravity in the range of 1.05 to 1.10.
Fluorocarbons	Impervious to water.
	With a refractive index close to that of water, it is claimed, makes them invisible to fish.
	Sinks quicker than nylon. Specific gravity in the range of 1.75 to 1.90.
	Knot strength is not as good as nylon.
	Generally harder than nylon, hence more abrasion resistant.
Wire	Resistant to bites and abrasions

Leader selection

As a general rule the butt diameter of a leader should be between 60% and 75% of the fly-line tip diameter.

The tippet size is determined by the size of the fish that are going to be caught. Also if a big or heavy fly is tied onto a thin tippet then there is a danger that it could snap off during casting. To have the best chance of catching a fish, the tippet should be as thin as possible.

Many commercial tippets are rated according to the X system but often they will state the diameter and breaking strength as well. The X scale runs from 8X (very fine) to 0X (thicker) tippet. From the X value it is possible to calculate the hook size that can be turned over by the tippet by multiplying it by 3 (some anglers use 4 depending on the air resistance of the fly).

The breaking strength can be determined by subtracting the X value from 9. Hence a 5X tippet will have a 4lb breaking limit. Diameter of the tippet in thousandths of an inch can be calculated by subtracting the X value from 11.

Care of leaders

Nylon monofilament degrades in UV so it should be stored away from daylight.

Make sure that knots are clinched and fully seated when they are tightened. They should be lubricated with moisture to prevent frictional heat from weakening the leader material as the knot is drawn together.

Poly-leaders

Often there is a requirement to fish sub-surface rather than using a floating leader and this can be achieved by using weighted flies, sinking fly-lines or sink-tips.

One of the most versatile methods for fishing at different depths is the poly-coated leader system. These are available in various lengths but are typically 10-15ft long. They can be joined together in different combinations such as an intermediate and then a fast sink depending on the depth at which fish are holding. Another alternative is to use an intermediate tip in front of the sinker to keep the fly off a river bed and hence avoid the likelihood of snagging the fly.

Poly-leaders and sink-tips are joined to the main fly-line with a loop-to-loop connection, which means that they are quickly interchangeable, one for another. The range of available sink rates includes:

- Floating
- Hover
- Intermediate
- Slow sink
- Fast sink
- Super fast sink
- Extra super fast sink

SAFETY CHECKLIST

General safety (SWEEP)		
	Hazard	**Precautions**
Suitable clothing	Eye Injury	Wear safety glasses or sun glasses
	Hook injury	Wear a hat
	Drowning	Use a safety vest or buoyancy aid
	Hypothermia	Wear appropriate clothing
	Sun burn/stroke	Apply high factor sun block and wear appropriate clothing
Weather	Extreme heat	Have plenty of drinks available
	Extreme cold	Wear lots of layers of clothing and thermal under garments
	Flooding	Mark water level and monitor it. Check weather forecast
	High winds	Use appropriate casting technique
	Cloud and mist	Be aware of route to safety
Electric shock	Lightning	Put fishing rods down immediately and do not stand under trees
	Electrical cables	Do not cast near to overhead electrical cables or supporting pylons/posts and avoid creating a path to earth through a fishing rod or fishing line
Environment	Slipping	Identify and advise hazardous areas
	Floating	Be aware of canoeists and floating debris
	People	Be aware of members of the public when back-casting
	River Authority	Be aware of by-laws and safety advice
	Accidents/illness	Check location of nearest Accident & Emergency hospital
Plants and Diseases	Giant Hogweed	Avoid contact which will cause running sores that take a very long time to heal (*see photo on opposite page*)
	Weil's disease	Water borne organism from rat's urine. Wash hands before eating food or touching mouth and eyes
	Zoonosis	Any infectious disease that can be transmitted (in some instances, by any agent i.e. person, animal or microorganism) from animals, both wild and domestic, to humans or from humans to animals (the latter is sometimes called reverse zoonosis or anthroponosis)
		Report any flu like symptoms to a doctor if they occur after fishing
	Lymes disease	Transmitted by ticks – do not get in close proximity to animals (e.g. deer and sheep)
	Algae	Do not swallow water and wash hands thoroughly
Always carry a mobile phone and advise someone where you are going, with a post code if possible, and what time you expect to return. In addition to 999 the EU emergency number is 112 and in the US it is 911.		

Giant Hogweed

General tackle handling		
	Hazard	**Precautions**
Hooks	Accidental penetration of hook into flesh	Use keeper ring or pass leader around the fly-reel and attach to one of the rod rings when carrying the rod to avoid an injury when walking, slipping or falling if the line or tippet gets snagged in the undergrowth
	Removing flies that are tangled up in bushes or trees	If fly cannot be removed by a roll cast, which often works, then wind as much fly-line back onto the reel as possible, turn away from the fly and apply tension gradually. Use extreme caution if this is the only solution and ensure that no part of your body is exposed to the fly should it catapult back.
	Windy conditions	Always make sure when casting that the fly is kept on the downwind side of the body
	Hook removal	Always seek medical assistance for hook removal

Stillwater safety		
	Hazard	**Precautions**
Boats	Bank anglers	Do not get closer than 50 metres to bank anglers
	Untidiness	Keep tackle neat and tidy
	Boarding and un-boarding	Always hold onto something on the shore side when getting in and out of boats
	Falling in the water	Avoid standing in the boat whilst fishing and leaning too far over the side
	High waves	Always steer the boat to cut through the waves straight-on and not side-on
	Strong winds	Check the weather forecast before starting out Fish in sheltered areas
	Sun burn/stroke	Apply high factor sun block taking special care to cover the ears and neck
	Unforeseen accident	Store the lodge phone number on your mobile phone
	Other craft	Powered boats must give way to non-powered boats Keep to the right (to starboard) when passing other craft Give way to any craft coming from the right (starboard) Maintain a distance of 50 metres from other craft
	Motors	Learn how to drive the boat before setting sail
	Propellers	Be careful not to snag drogues and lines in the propeller when motoring
	Shear pins	Don't go into shallow water because this could cause the shear-pin (which protects the propeller) to break
	Docking	Be sure to cut the engine and cruise for the last few metres
	Alcohol	Never drink alcohol when in a boat
	Comfort	Always use a boat seat or thwart board
Wading	Quicksand	Be aware of any quicksands or deep mud around the water
Back casts	In boats	Be careful not to hook your boat partner Cast over the opposite side if possible especially in high winds Be aware of other boats in the vicinity Be aware of members of the public on the shore
	On the bank	Be aware of other anglers, animals and members of the public in the vicinity
Make sure you have the lodge phone number in your mobile phone before setting out		

River safety		
	Hazard	**Precautions**
Banks	Slipping	Take care when climbing up and down river banks
	Undercut collapse	Never stand on banks that have been undercut by the river because they can collapse without warning
	Undergrowth	Never tread on undergrowth unless you know what is underneath it. Often there are hidden holes or a drop into the river
	Wet mud	Don't walk on wet mud; it is always slippery
Wading	Unfamiliar riverbed	Always use a wading staff to give extra support and to prevent falls It is very dangerous to put hands out when falling into the river because it is not possible to judge the characteristics of riverbed below the surface (rocks, sharp stones, holes etc.) Wear Polaroid glasses which allow obstacles to be seen under the water
	Rocks	Always keep one foot on the riverbed when clambering over rocks because there could be hidden traps below the water's surface Tops of rocks might be slippery and so it is advisable not to stand on them
	Sand bars	Always make sure that you can wade out of a sand bar because often they end with a steep drop-off – it may be difficult to wade back up the sand bar against the current
	Slab rock	Wear felt soles on wading boots instead or as well as studs. Note that felt is not suitable for walking on rocks or mud
	Holes	Be careful of drop-offs and get guidance as to where these are likely to be. Where possible only wade where the riverbed is visible
	Floating debris	Be alert for logs and other debris floating downstream
	Canoeists	Be alert for canoeists and direct them to where you would like them to pass
	Strong currents	Always wade side-on against the current and use a wading stick. It is easier to wade diagonally downstream and in shallow riffles. Do not cross your legs when wading. If the water gets too deep for comfort wade backwards upstream
	Tree roots	Be careful of submerged roots, wire and briars which can cause tripping or entanglement
	Wire and briars	
	High banks	Before entering the water make sure that there is a way out further down-stream

River safety		
Falling in	Waders filling up with water	Always wear a wading belt which will prevent water entering the lower half of the waders. Remember that the waders are full of air which the water cannot easily displace if you have the legs high
	In shallow water	Waders will be full of air and will float. Back paddle back to where it is possible to get onto the knees and stand up
	In deep water	Roll over on your back, stretch out arms and float, feet first with the toes out of the water, downstream, to where there is an easy place to crawl out onto the river bank. Focus on the landing point and use the outstretched arms as oars for guidance. Do not try to lift yourself out of the water by using tree branches that may not take your weight. Empty out waders before attempting to stand up. Take care not to get trapped under overhanging objects.

© US National Library of Medicine (NLM)

We don't want this to happen!

Bibiography

Title and Author	Publisher	ISBN Number
Presentation by Gary A Borger	Tomorrow River Press	ISBN 0 962839 25 6
Fly Fishing Outside the Box by Peter Hayes	Coch-y-Bonddu Books	ISBN 978 1 904784 56 2
A Guide to Aquatic Trout Food by Dave Whitlock	Swan Hill Press	ISBN 1 853105 08 2
Trout Flies of Britain and Europe by John Goddard	A & C Black	ISBN 0 713634 46 4
The Pocket Guide to Matching the Hatch by Peter Lapsley and Cyril Bennett	Merlin Unwin Books	ISBN 978 1 906122 20 1
Still Water Fly Fishing for Trout by Chris James	Robert Hale	ISBN 0 709052 70 7
A Guide to River Trout Flies by John Roberts	The Crowood Press	ISBN 1 852239 36 0
Trout from a Boat by Dennis Moss	Merlin Unwin Books	ISBN 978 1 906122 53 9
Micropatterns by Darrel Martin	Swan Hill Press	ISBN 1 853105 42 2
Tactical Fly Fishing by Jeremy Lucas	Crowood Press	ISBN 978 1 847971 26 5

INDEX

Adams	38
Amber sedge	50
backing	4, 6
Black buzzer	23, 30
Blob	30
Blood knot	18
tucked	19
Bloodworm	23
boat fly patterns	30
Booby	31
braided loop	20
buzzers	22
Caddis imitation	50
Caddis patterns	52
caddisflies	51
Cascade	67
Cat's whisker	16
chironomids	23
Claret hopper	23, 30
cofilaments	78
Collie dog	67
copolymers	78
Czech nymph	52
Czech nymphing	44, 47, 50, 51
Daddy longlegs	16
Damsel nymphs	16
Davy knot	33
depths, fishing at	31
Diawl bach	23, 30
diptera	23
Double blood knot	42
Double blood knot	52
Double turle knot	72
drag-free drift	39, 58
drifting	28
drogue	28, 29
droppers	32
sliding and rotating	52
dry fly fishing	36
dry fly patterns	38
dry fly, presentation of	39
duns	37
Elk hair sedge	50, 52
emerger	37
ephemeroptera	37
feeding lanes	40
Figure-of-eight dropper	35
Figure-of-eight loop	34
fishing depth	27
fluorocarbons	78
fly-line	3
fly-reel	2
fly-rod	2
flycasting	54
Flycasting Skills	56
French nymphing	47
g-clamps	28
Gold-ribbed hare's ear	46, 64
Greenwell's glory	38
Grey duster	38
Grey sakasa kebari	64
Grinner knot	4, 5, 52, 53
Heavy nymph	46
Hot pink booby	30
imago	37
Ishigaki kebari	64
Klinkhamer	50, 52, 53
dryfly	53
landing trout	17
leaders	27, 32, 78
bioabsorbal polymer	78
care of	79
furled	78
light intensity	27
polycoated	78
set-up (wet fly)	32

leader lengths (for nymphing) 47
Lilian knot 62
locating salmon 68
locating trout 14
loch-style 22
long-bellied Spey line 71
loop-to-loop connection 76
lure fishing 12
mayflies 37
midges 23
Muddler minnow 16
multi-tip Spey line 71
Nail knot 7
New Zealand style 53
nymph fishing 44
   nymphs 37
   nymph patterns 46
nymphing rig 45
Orange quill 38
overhead cast 57
paradrogue 28, 29
perfection loop 41
Pheasant tail nymph 46, 53
Pink shrimp 46
playing rainbow trout 24
Polish nymphing 44, 47
poly-leaders 79
Pot bellied pig 67
reading the river 48
reservoir boat fishing 22
retrieval 27
river trout lies 40
river trout lies 49
Roll cast 55
Royal coachman sakasa kebari 64
royal wulff 38
safety 80-84
salmon fishing 66

salmon flies 67
salmon lies 69
seasons 26
sedge 51
shooting heads 70, 71, 76
shooting heads 74
Silver stoat 67
sink-tips 79
Skagit line 71, 75
Soldier palmer 50
Spanish nymphing 47
Spey lines 70
spinner 37
stillwater patterns 16
stony riverbeds 50
Stopper knot 53
tapered leaders 3, 39, 41
Tenkara 60
   fly patterns 64
   rigs 62
   rods 61
time of day 26
tippet 3
trichoptera 51
Tungsten-head pheasant tail nymph 46, 53
upwinged flies 37
Viva 16
washing line style 31
water temperature 27
weather 26
welded loop 76, 77
whipped loop 10, 11, 39
Willy Gunn (tube fly) 67

Flycasting Skills
John Symonds £9.99

Trout from a Boat
Dennis Moss £16

Pocket Guide to Matching the Hatch
Peter Lapsley and Cyril Bennett £7.99

Pocket Guide to Fishing Knots
Step-by-Step Coarse, Sea and Game Knots
Peter Owen £5.99

Beginner's Guide to Flytying
Chris Mann and Terry Griffiths £9.99

**Complete Illustrated Directory
of Salmon Flies**
Chris Mann £20

Trout in Dirty Places
Theo Pike £20

Once a Flyfisher
Laurence Catlow £17.99

The Fisherman's Bedside Book
BB £18.95

Canal Fishing
Dominic Garnett £20

Flyfishing for Coarse Fish
Dominic Garnett £20

Fishing with Harry
Tony Baws £15.99

Fishing with Emma
David Overland £9.99

www.merlinunwin.co.uk